STARTING OUT

IN

GOLF

STARTING OUT
IN
GOLF

CollinsWillow
An Imprint of HarperCollins*Publishers*

First published in 1992 by
Collins Willow
an imprint of HarperCollins Publishers
London

©SP Creative Design 1992

A CIP catalogue for this book is
available from the British Library

ISBN 0 00 218 422 2

Designed and produced by
SP Creative Design
Linden House, Kings Road, Bury St Edmunds, Suffolk
Art Director: Rolando Ugolini
Editor: Heather Thomas

Photographs by Mark Shearman,
Bob Thomas Sports Photography and Allsport

Typeset in Stone Serif by Halcyon Type & Design, Ipswich, Suffolk
Colour origination by J Film Process Company Ltd, Bangkok
Printed and bound in Italy by New Interlitho SpA, Milan

Contents

Nigel Blenkarne

Nigel Blenkarne has 18 years experience as a professional golfer. He became PGA qualified in 1977 and earned his European Tour Players card finishing third behind Sandy Lyle. After three years playing full time in Europe and South Africa, he became club professional at Salisbury, later moving on to the picturesque Parkstone Golf Club in Dorset, and in 1992 was appointed Director of Golf at Bowood Golf and Country Club, Wiltshire.

Nigel's teaching ability has made him well known and sought after, and he coaches a number of successful tournament professionals. He has written and co-presented the video *Golf for Women* with pupil Diane Barnard, a winner on the WPG European Tour.

Jim Christine

Jim Christine is the golf professional at Worplesdon Golf Club, Surrey. He is a Senior Swing Tutor with the PGA and a *Golf World* magazine teaching panellist since 1987. He is also a regular teacher at *Golf World* schools. He is coach to the English Girls National team and has considerable experience of coaching juniors and beginners.

Craig DeFoy

Craig DeFoy is the golf professional at Combe Hill Golf Club, Surrey. He was a tournament player on the European circuit for many years and has won several tournaments. He has represented Wales seven times in the World Cup, and Britain twice in the PGA Cup. He is now the Welsh National Coach.

Martin Vousden

Martin Vousden is the deputy editor of *Today's Golfer* magazine. He writes regular features on the Rules of Golf for the magazine and has also written a book on the subject. His great regret is that he did not take up golf until his late twenties, but he now plays regularly and has a handicap of 12.

CHAPTER ONE

Preparing to play

by Nigel Blenkarne

Welcome to the wonderful game of golf, which has often been labelled, quite correctly, 'the game of a lifetime'. Golf has a marvellous flexibility and allows players of all ages and abilities to enjoy the game and play together due to the equitable handicap system.

Whilst a round of golf takes about four hours, you have the option of playing with one, two or three other players; you may decide to play nine or even six holes if time is against you, provided that the course layout and club rules permit the playing of part rounds. Or you may hit practice balls or fine tune your putting stroke on the practice green for just a few minutes.

There are many reasons why we play golf and which make it so popular:
● Social: it is very conducive to conversation, both during and after the round.
● Exercise: in beautiful surroundings, it involves a four to five mile walk without any danger or risks as in some other sports.
● Competition: it can be arranged in many different formats.
● Travel: there aren't many places in the world without golf courses.
● Business: many valued contacts have been made on golf courses. The game also lends itself to hospitality and entertaining.

In addition to all this, golf presents you with a permanent challenge and almost infinite variations each time you play – the weather, course conditions, new obstacles and hazards. And even your own ability will fluctuate considerably from your best to your worst performance. These are just some of the factors that combine to make golf so wonderfully unpredictable. Perhaps the best example at the highest level is Jack Nicklaus' first and second rounds in the 1985 Open at Royal St Georges when he scored 83-66. The same man, same clubs, same course, different weather conditions but he found the game more to his liking on the second day.

You will have days when hitting the golf ball seems a comparatively easy thing to do and other days when it feels awkward and difficult. The information and knowledge, gained over many years, given in this book will help you make your good days better and the bad ones less bad, both resulting in a more enjoyable game of golf. Good luck.

Preparing to play

Equipment

There is a massive amount of choice now on the market, and it can be a very confusing task trying to select your golf clubs particularly from the enormous range available.

Contrary to some beliefs, it is not necessary to spend a fortune equipping yourself to get started in golf, although you can if you wish! A used half set can be quite adequate, provided that the clubs are suitable for your build, and can be obtained for a modest sum.

The PGA Professional you choose for your first lessons is the obvious person to guide you in selecting the right equipment for you. He will be keen for you to become a long-term customer and will look after your needs as you progress in the game. Beware of an apparent bargain which will have no value to you if it doesn't suit you!

To most people starting out, all golf clubs appear the same, but there are a number of characteristics in the construction of a club that need to be taken into consideration when selecting your new set, whether it be a full set, half set or just an individual club to start you off.

We are all built differently and being fitted correctly for your golf clubs is similar to choosing well-fitting clothes. Overall height, arm length, leg length, body length, hand size, strength and natural rhythm are the major factors that will influence the way you stand and swing the club and therefore the type of club you should use. When

advising you on which clubs to buy, your Professional will take the following into account:
- Lie of the club
- Loft and shaft length
- Grip thickness
- Weight distribution and club head design
- Shaft flexibility
- Overall weight and swingweight

Lie of the club

This is the angle between the sole of the club head and the shaft. It is particularly important to have the lie of the iron clubs correct because with these clubs you should take a divot, and if the lie is not right, either the heel or the toe of the club will dig into the ground causing the club head to twist at impact. Throughout a set of irons the lie angle will vary due to the shaft of the club graduating in length.

Most irons are designed with a slightly curved sole so that at the address position the heel and the toe cannot both touch the ground. It is preferable to have the toe just off the ground with the sole sitting between the heel and the centre of the club. This is because the force of the swing causes the shaft to bow outwards slightly during the return swing.

Your height and arm length will determine whether you will need standard lie clubs or not. If you are tall and your fingertips are more than 29 inches from the ground when standing erect, then you will require your clubs to be more upright than standard. Conversely, if you are short and the fingertip to the ground measurement is less than 27 inches you will need flatter lie clubs.

If you fall into either of these categories it is important to seek professional advice to help you adopt firstly the correct posture in your set up and then establish the necessary degree of alteration from standard.

Loft and shaft lengths

Golf clubs fall into two distinct groups – woods and irons. Woods are now constructed from a number of hi-tech materials including stainless steel, alloy, graphite, ulremid plastic, copper berylium and even titanium. Stainless steel is the most popular although some better players still prefer the natural feel of the solid block of persimmon wood.

The loft of the face and the length of the shaft vary with each club. From the no. 1 wood (driver) to the pitching wedge, the loft angle increases from approximately 10 degrees to a backward slant of around 50 degrees. As the loft increases by increments of four degrees the shaft length decreases by ½ inch per club in each of the groups, the shortest wood shaft being about three inches longer than the longest iron shaft.

Above: Here you can see three 5 iron clubs which are available in flat, standard and upright lie options. Notice how the soles of all three clubs are sitting flat on the ground.

Preparing to play

Grip thickness

This will be determined by the size of your hands and length of your fingers. Ladies' grips are therefore the thinnest, whereas specially manufactured Jumbo grips are the thickest. The Jumbo grip is designed for people with large hands but is also very beneficial for the older player who suffers from arthritis and finds it difficult to close the fingers. Your club grip can be packed to the correct thickness for you, and again you should seek the advice of your teaching Professional.

You should aim to have the fingers of your left hand just touching the

Above: How to find the correct grip thickness. The finger should just meet the fleshy part of the thumb joint (top left). A space (above right) or the thumb joint overlapping the fingers (above) are both unsuitable.

fleshy part of your thumb joint when they are closed around the grip. The right hand should then feel able to hold the grip in the fingers and fall with the fleshy part of the right thumb joint on top of the left thumb.

A grip that is too thin will cause the fingertips to dig into the palm of your hand, while too thick a grip will not allow your fingers to close properly around it.

Weight distribution and club head design

In the last 15 years we have seen a major change in the design of the club head; through research and development manufacturers have discovered that the majority of amateur golfers will perform better with a heel, toe and sole weighted club head. Because the novice golfer and even the regular club player are not likely to strike the ball right in the centre of the club face all the time it is therefore a benefit to have the weight distributed around the perimeter of the club head. This has the effect of making the sweet spot bigger and will allow you to get away with an off centre hit better than if you used a blade club.

There is still a very considerable demand for blade clubs, which have a more classic appearance with clean lines as opposed to the chunky rounded edges of most perimeter weighted clubs. The blade club is favoured by the purist golfer, the lower-handicap player and by professionals, all of whom are generally more proficient golfers who have learned a better technique and strike the ball in the centre of the club most of the time. Arguably, the blade type club gives a more satisfying feel of strike when played correctly.

Iron club heads are manufactured in two ways – either cast or forged – and each has its own merits. As a learner you are better to start with a cast club because the steel is harder and more durable and requires less careful maintenance.

The more advanced player may benefit from forged clubs because these are made of a mild steel which gives a softer feel and more controlled ball flight, but set against this is the fact they will dent and mark much more easily, especially if used on a stony course.

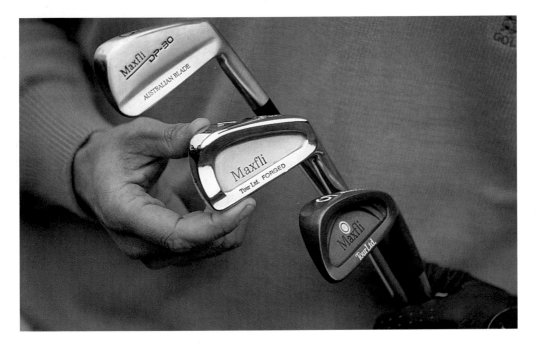

Three distinctly different designs of iron heads. From the top: a forged blade; a forged heel and toe weighted club; and cast heel and toe weighted (harder steel).

Preparing to play

Shaft flexibility

Generally the range of shaft flexes available are: ladies, flexible mens, regular, stiff and extra stiff. However, different club manufacturers have their own methods of measuring and grading the shafts they use. Therefore one company's regular shaft may equate to a stiff one in another make.

The shaft is the guts of the golf club which transfers the power of your swing to the club head. It is your physical strength, hand action and speed of swing that will determine which flex is most suitable for you. A slow swing will be better suited to more flexible shafts; if you are strong with a fast swing, then a stiffer shaft will help you.

As an example, if an older player with a slow swing uses too stiff a shaft the ball will probably go fairly straight but will lack distance. On the other hand, a strong swinger using a very flexible shaft may hit the ball a very long way but without any control over direction.

It is the correct balance between distance and accuracy that you should be aiming for when choosing the right shaft flex. As a learner it may be too early to know whether you tend to hit the ball high or low, but it is worth explaining briefly that the shaft can now be made to bend most at a low flex point, i.e. nearer the club head, which will help you hit the ball higher. Alternatively, a high flex point, which is nearer to the grip of the club, will tend to produce a lower ball flight.

This factor is slightly advanced for the beginner but it is worth starting to understand how the flex of the shaft affects the ball flight. Most learners are better with a low flex point because it encourages them to get the ball airborne.

Overall weight and swing-weight

The overall weight of the club is the dead weight, or total weight, of all the components. The swingweight is the balance between the club head weight related to the weight of the grip and shaft. As the name implies, this is the measurement of the club head's weight which you actually feel when you swing the club.

Swingweights are measured in scales from A to D and within each letter from 0 - 9 (lightest to heaviest). The A and B scales should be disregarded as they are ultra light and not to be recommended unless you have an unusually weak swing. The standard range for ladies is between C4 - C7, and for men between D0 - D2. A set of clubs should all be matched for swingweight.

There is an element of personal preference in choosing weight but it is likely to be influenced by the speed of the swing and not so much purely by physical strength. For example, two of the world's best ever golfers and both strong men, Jack Nicklaus and Arnold Palmer, both use clubs of very different swingweights. Nicklaus who has a slow swing uses C9 clubs, whereas Palmer, with a more brisk swing, plays with D5 swingweight clubs. A naturally fast swing needs the extra club head weight or otherwise it is likely to become just too fast.

The weight of the club head will influence how the shaft flexes. A standard, regular shaft will flex more with a heavy club head at the end of it than a light one. Also the length of the shaft influences the swingweight, so if you are short and require a shorter than standard shaft it will make the swing-weight lighter unless other adjustments are made – self-adhesive lead tape is available for this purpose.

As you probably realise by now, all these factors are linked and affect each other. Whilst it is not essential to have custom-fitted clubs when you first start, it is very important to get the lie, grip thickness and shaft flex correct at the beginning. Even if you decide on one or two clubs or a second-hand set, ask your pro to advise you on what best suits your build and natural method.

Pitching wedge and sand wedge

If you decide to start with a half set of clubs you will probably have either a pitching wedge or a sand wedge but not both. However, it is worth noting the difference in design of these two clubs and the purpose they are required to perform.

The pitching wedge has a flat, narrow sole with a straighter leading edge to help you get a crisp contact with the ball even from a hard bare lie.

The sand wedge sole is heavier, more rounded and the back edge of the sole is lower than the front leading edge. This is to help the club bounce through

the sand and not dig in too deeply which a pitching wedge tends to do. The sand wedge is the heaviest club head in a set, and it encourages the club to keep

moving through the sand and the ball.

Although its name implies that it is used mainly in bunkers, the sand wedge may also be used from grass, but beware as you will need some soft grass underneath the ball. From a hard bare lie, it is not advisable to use the sand wedge because its sole will tend to bounce and you would then catch the ball very thin.

Putters

Selecting a putter is a very personal choice as there are hundreds of different designs available, ranging from traditional shapes to some very weird and wonderful ones. Unlike the rest of your clubs there is no right or wrong; it is simply finding the one that works best for you. If you can get the ball in the hole and you are confident with any design of putter, then use it.

This shows the difference between a sand wedge and a pitching wedge. Notice the space under the front edge of the sand wedge (left). It sits on the flange at the back of the sole whereas the pitching wedge has a flat sole to allow the leading front edge to be on the ground.

Preparing to play

This is the golf club you will use most in a round and is therefore perhaps the most important one in your bag. Most established golfers have two or three spare putters because inevitably the old faithful will misbehave occasionally and confidence will fade and that is the time for a change, even for a short period. Then when you return to your favourite again, it will feel a lot better.

Many top professionals have used dozens of different putters during their careers although some have stuck to one in the belief that if it has performed well in the past it cannot be the fault of the tool if they sometimes miss putts.

Putter shaft lengths can vary from 32 inches to 36 inches, so it is worth considering this if you happen to be tall or short. But remember that a shorter shaft will make the head weight feel lighter, and a longer shaft increases the feel of the head weight.

It is also a good idea to choose a putter with a lie angle that allows you to keep the sole of the putter flat, and you should also stand so that your eye line is over the ball.

A recent trend is the introduction of the very long-shafted putter which is held with the top of the grip against either your chin or chest, and the hands split by up to 18 inches. Although these putters have been the saviour of quite a number of Tour players I would not recommend them to a beginner. It is worth trying the 'broom handle' length putter only if you have persevered with a standard length and really struggled.

Some of the most popular styles of putters. From left to right: blade putter with flange; mild steel putter with milled head, heel and toe weighted; centre shaft, brass head (this may be used by right or left handers); mallet head with lines; black head, heel and toe weighted with sighting lines.

Bags

You must decide first whether you want to use a trolley or carry your clubs before you can select a bag, and although some bags can double for both purposes this is never very satisfactory.

If you wish to use a trolley, particularly an electric one, then the size of bag you have can be larger allowing more storage space for your clubs and clothing. Many learners feel rather conspicuous with a large bag and prefer a lightweight carrying bag. This option is more sensible if you are not starting off with a full set.

A full set of clubs requires the base of the bag to be large enough to let all the grips fit without jamming and making it difficult to remove each club, which is not only annoying but can also cause damage to the grips. Some bags now have dividers that continue down halfway or right to the base which is a good way to avoid clubs jamming.

Trolleys

Golf trolleys fall into two groups: hand pull or electric motorized. Of the pull types there are those that fold up keeping the bag attached and those that require the bag to be removed first.

Bag stands

During the damp winter months when the ground is often wet with dew it is a good idea to consider using a bag stand on your carrybag.

Shoes

It is important to realise that you will walk about four miles during an average round of golf so it is crucial that you have a comfortable pair of shoes.

1 All leather shoes are very comfortable once they have been worn a few times and broken in, but they should not be worn too often in wet conditions.

2 A man-made sole, leather upper shoe is a good all-year-round shoe provided that you keep the leather clean and polished.

3 The leather upper shoe with a waterproof membrane is an ideal combination of breathability and waterproofing which make it good all-year-round.

4 The synthetic shoe ranges from an inexpensive plastic or rubber, through poromeric to some modern synthetic materials which you are hard-pressed to tell apart from leather.

5 The athletic style is a fairly recent trend for golf shoes, and these shoes are styled more in the mould of a training shoe. They are usually very light and comfortable.

6 Metal spikes are fitted to the majority of golf shoes. Some are metal combined with a nylon plate which reduces the overall weight of the shoe.

7 Rubber studs became popular in the early 1980s when approximately 70 per cent of golfers favoured them. They are very comfortable, especially when the ground is hard, but should be avoided when the ground is soft.

Gloves

Most golfers prefer to wear a glove on the upper hand, i.e. the left hand for a right-handed player. It helps to give adhesion especially at the top of the

Preparing to play

backswing and at impact in the event of a mishit.

Leather gloves are traditional and are still favoured by many golfers as giving the most sensitive feel in dry conditions.

Synthetic gloves not only look and feel like leather but they also perform very well, cost less, last longer and are good in wet conditions.

All weather gloves were originally gloves that were not very good in dry conditions. However, with the recent improvements made to synthetic materials, they now perform very well when dry or wet.

Clothing

You should wear comfortable clothes which allow you to move without restriction. They should not be too tight nor too loose and flappy. To play your best golf you need to look and feel comfortable in your clothes.

Certain standards of dress are expected at most golf clubs and as a learner you will feel much more at ease if you dress in the accepted fashion. Acceptable levels do vary, and municipal courses are not so particular as private clubs.

Waterproof clothing

In the United Kingdom, this is another important item for the serious golfer to consider. If you are a fairweather player, that's fine, but it will restrict the number of days you can play and, given the right waterproof clothing, the game is still enjoyable in very wet conditions.

Goretex membrane has been used in mountaineering, ski wear and golfing for some time, and is the most breathable and waterproof fabric on the market. It has millions of tiny pores which are small enough not to allow water droplets in the form of rain to penetrate, and yet the pores are large enough to allow water vapour to escape thereby allowing your body to breathe.

Other breathable waterproof membranes are used to produce mid-price range suits or you may just want a nylon suit which will keep you dry in emergencies without costing very much.

Whichever type you choose make sure that you never leave a wet suit in your bag after playing, and make a habit of storing your suit separately.

The following points are worth noting when buying a suit:
● Arms should be long enough so that when you fully extend your arms the cuffs do not ride up.
● The overlap of the jacket over the top of the trousers should be at least 9 inches.
● You should have some surplus material free under your arm to allow for your body turn.
● The bottoms of the waterproof trousers should overlap the top of your shoes by at least two inches.
● The brim of a waterproof hat should overlap your jacket collar when it is turned up.
● Trousers with built-in pockets are preferable to those with slits.
● Consider how much noise the fabric makes when you move; it should not annoy you during your swing.

Golf balls

These can be split into two distinct groups as follows:

1 Two piece, solid core.

2 Wound, three piece construction.

Two piece balls are preferable for the learner because they are very durable and have a lower spin rate which will maximize the roll distance and also minimize any side spin you may impart which causes hooked or sliced shots. Their disadvantage is that they will not stop so quickly on the green.

Wound balls are available with two types of cover: surlyn (man-made) or natural balata. A wound balata ball is the ultimate performance ball for many better players but it is not recommended for the average player. Surlyn wound balls offer control and feel characteristics that are similar to a balata ball but are also much more durable.

Most wound balls are available in two compression options – 90 or 100 – which are a measurement of a golf ball's resistance to impact force. A lower compression ball will flatten against the club face to a greater degree than a higher compression ball subjected to the same impact. A player generating a lot of club head speed will favour the 100 compression ball, feeling that the 90 compression ball will be too soft at impact.

Bear in mind also that all golf balls are affected considerably by temperature. A warm ball will be more springy and will therefore compress more easily and travel further than a cold ball, which feels harder and is less able to compress. Therefore you must take temperature into consideration when you are judging distance.

Caring for your clubs and equipment

To ensure that your set of golf clubs stays looking good and working for you with maximum efficiency, a few basic and easy-to-follow tips should be noted:

● Always wipe any dirt off the face of the club with a towel after each shot.

● Wipe the ball clean before teeing off on each hole.

● Occasionally use a groove scraping tool and brush to remove any dirt from the club face grooves.

● Always keep head covers on your woods, even if they are of metal construction. Iron covers are also available and are a good idea for graphite shaft irons.

● Do not leave your clubs wet after play – always dry them.

Any dirt on either the ball or the club face will result in an abrasive action on both surfaces at impact and will adversely affect the club face and could cause an inconsistent flight of the ball. This applies especially to your wooden clubs even if they are of metal construction.

Preparing to play

Taking lessons

You should not rush straight to the course and expect to be able to play the game. You need some time to learn the correct basic skills away from the course on a driving range or practice ground.

Obviously, to do this you need to be taught the right things to practise, and as a teacher it is always preferable to start a beginner off absolutely from scratch before any bad habits have been learned. Many beginners have tried a few games with a friend, realised that golf is not easy and then sought the services of a golf professional, who has to undo some faults before introducing the correct fundamentals of golfing technique.

Go in person to your local PGA professional to ask if he or she or an assistant would be prepared to teach you from scratch, and you will instantly know if there is a genuine interest and enthusiasm to teach you the game. Some professionals specialize in other areas and don't particularly enjoy teaching; if that is the case seek out another professional who you feel has a genuine desire to help you. You must feel confident and at ease with your teacher and be able to communicate and understand him. It's not like going to have your car tyres changed so do try and choose a professional with whom you can develop a good relationship. Once you have found the professional who makes you feel confident, then ask for his advice on the best equipment for you; he will help you with every aspect of learning golf if you are loyal and support his golf shop.

Don't forget that the professional is a human being with just the same emotions and feelings as you. He may be shy or slightly nervous initially but you need to be happy that he can impart the knowledge you are seeking. So don't be afraid to ask lots of questions about the game, the club, the Rules of golf and how long he has been a professional. The new golfer needs to be like a sponge soaking up as much information as possible.

Try and have your first six lessons closely grouped; perhaps one or two per week to give yourself a chance to grasp a consistent set up and basic swing which can move the ball with some reliability before you attempt playing a round of golf. Also practise as much as you can between lessons to train your golf muscles with exercises and swings. Learning a good swing early on is just as important, if not more so, than the equipment you buy, and it is sensible to invest a large percentage of your financial outlay on tuition and, if necessary, economize on your golf clubs. Don't go hunting for the cheapest lessons you can find because they will almost certainly not be very good.

Group tuition is an interesting and inexpensive method of getting started. Many professionals run evening classes during the winter at local sports halls, but remember that you are sharing the professional's attention with other

people, and, if you can afford it, a one-to-one relationship or smaller group will give you the best chance to learn more quickly.

Whichever way you choose to learn, be patient for the first two to three months. Golf cannot be learned overnight, and as long as you play you can still improve provided that you are reasonably fit. It is worth going back to your professional for checking even after you have developed a sound swing in order to avoid slipping back into any bad habits. There is no limit to the number of lessons any golfer should have, whatever his ability and experience.

Preparing to play

Exercises

Warming-up exercises

You should never go straight to the first tee and play without performing some loosening movements to stretch out your muscles gently before hitting the ball in earnest. Ideally, you should allow yourself time to hit 20 or so practice balls before playing, starting with some short wedge or 9-iron shots and working up to the long clubs finishing with a few drives. However, if time prohibits this, try and use these warm-up exercises to help get your golf muscles ready to operate.

Club shaft across shoulders

Adopt a normal correct stance and posture, holding a club shaft across your shoulders by crossing your forearms and pressing the shaft against your shoulders as high as possible with your fingers. It is best to have your left forearm crossing over your right arm. Notice that the shaft line points up slightly with the left shoulder higher than the right.

Now push the right shoulder back with your left hand until the shaft line has turned through 90 degrees. Remember to keep your eyes focused on a point so that your head remains steady but keep on holding your chin up to allow a free turn. Then turn your shoulders in the opposite direction allowing your hips and right knee and foot to move across to the left as in a normal swing. The opposite end of the club shaft should now be pointing at the same spot as on the backswing turn, but please note that this point should not be where the ball position should be but approximately six feet away from you.

Whilst performing this exercise, you should feel your weight being transferred onto your right leg on the backswing turn, and your left leg on the follow through position as should be the case in a correct golf swing.

Posture reminder

Hold a golf club at the head end with your right hand, standing erect. Hold the club shaft against your back from the base of your spine to the back of your head. Then bend forwards from your hips, keeping the club shaft against your spine with your chin up and your left arm hanging freely away from your body.

This spine angle is one of the most important factors of the set up and will influence your swing later.

Club shaft across hips

Hold the club shaft in your fingers with both hands spread the width of your hips and with your thumbs pointing inwards. Hold the club shaft across your hips with the thumbs resting against each hip joint.

Make the backswing turn by pushing your right hip back, and similarly on the follow through, push your left hip back with your left thumb. The object of this exercise is to feel your hips moving in a rotational, not a sideways, action. Be aware of your weight on the right leg on the backswing transferring to the left leg on the follow through.

Swing two clubs

Take your two longest irons (2 and 3, 3 and 4) and hold both clubs together using a two-handed grip. Then swing them together slowly and feel your body turn and stretch. Start with short swings back and forth, then gradually lengthen them until you arrive at your full swing. Do not attempt to swing hard. It will be impossible to swing quickly because of the additional weight.

Fit for golf exercises

There are three elements that the golfer can develop to improve his or her golf. These are as follows:
1 Strength
2 Flexibility
3 Muscular endurance, which includes general health.

Strength is essential to produce distance but it must be allied to a supple flexible body to reach certain positions that allow for full use of the muscular strength available.

Muscular endurance means that the muscles can still perform efficiently even after many holes of golf, while a healthy heart and lungs will help prevent you tiring easily.

Many men tend to lose flexibility as they get older which restricts their ability to turn fully on the swing resulting in a loss of power. Women do become less flexible as they age, but lack of strength is the factor that most restricts their club head speed and thereby distance.

You will have to assess your own strengths and weaknesses to decide which exercises will benefit you most.

The general areas on which to concentrate are: hands, forearms, trunk rotation, back, abdomen and legs.

Strength in your fingers, hands and wrists will help you to control the golf club. Use a grip squeezer, especially in your left hand (because most right-handed players are much weaker in their left hands). This is one of the best and easiest ways to improve these important golf muscles. Equal strength in each hand is ideal, but not often found.

The golf swing is a rotary movement, so any exercise to emphasize the rotation of the trunk is very beneficial. For most people, just a few minutes a day practising some of the suggested exercises would help considerably in toning their bodies as well as gently and gradually increasing strength. They would benefit your health and your golf game. However, don't overdo it; build a programme for you that trains, not strains. For example, five of these exercises repeated 10 times each would be enough for most people initially. Increase or decrease the number of repetitions according to what feels comfortable for you.

Preparing to play

The lunge

Alternate your legs and bend both knees at an angle of 90 degrees. The lower knee should not quite touch the ground.

Arm support running

Supporting all your weight with your arms, spring your legs forward alternately so that your knee touches your elbow on each thrust.

Salmon snaps

Start off lying on your back with your arms extended behind you. Raise your legs straight up by bending from the hips. Bring your hands up to touch as near to your ankles as possible.

Upper torso lift

Lie down with your hands held together under your chin. Raise your shoulders, arms and hands a few inches, keeping your legs together on the ground. Hold for a few seconds and then lower.

Side torso lift

Support your body weight on the elbow of one arm, and place your other arm across the front of your body to hold your lower hip. Keep your legs together, resting on the outer edge of the lower foot. Now lift your hips until your body is in a straight line. Hold for a few seconds, then lower.

Back to the wall

Adopt a sitting position, keeping your back straight and pressed against a wall. Make a 90 degrees bend at your hips and knees. Hold the position for 10 seconds.

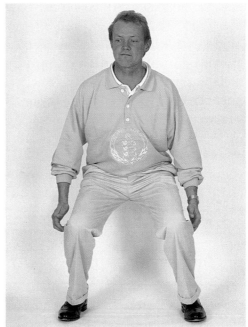

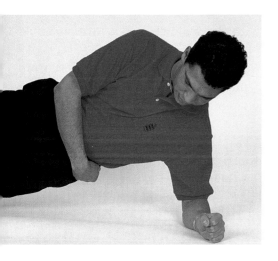

Elbow to knee cross-over ▼

Lie on your back with your hands behind your head. Lift your left knee up and bring your right elbow forward to touch it. Then alternate with the right knee to the left elbow.

Rubber tube stretch ▶

Using a length of flexible rubber tube, stand it on end and hold the other end at shoulder height, keeping the tube taut. Now straighten your arm as if punching the ceiling.

Leg lift

Lying face down on the ground, lift your legs together a few inches off the floor from the hips. Hold for a few seconds, then lower.

Preparing to play

Practice

The purpose of practice is to tell the brain as accurately as possible how to organize the movements of the body. To practise constructively you must have the right thoughts in your mind. Aimlessly hitting balls on the practice ground or driving range is nothing more than a physical exercise; it will not improve your game and may even do damage.

Golf is a target game, so practice should always include targets. Make your practice as similar as possible to the real thing – actual play. Your aim and alignment are always crucial factors; if they are not correct, then your swing will compensate with faults. Always check that your thoughts and reality correspond by placing some clubs on the ground to check your feet, club face and ball positions (you are not permitted to do this on the course).

Once you have a target and aim, then try to visualize the shot you are practising: imagine the flight of the ball in your mind. How high is the flight? Where will the ball land? How much roll will it have? Set yourself competitive goals; for example, hitting seven out of ten bunker shots on to the green, or eight out of ten drives between two target trees. Play a number of chips and putts from different positions around the green and see how many times you can get down in two.

Never practise hitting the ball flat out with any club; it is far better and promotes control and feel to practise half shots and three-quarter shots, and then hit two different lofted clubs the same distance. For example, hit ten 8 iron shots, then switch to a 6 iron and hit 10 balls the same distance, but always to a target. You will soon begin to realise the distance that can be achieved with little effort. Don't always practise with the same clubs but introduce lots of variation.

Immediately after a lesson from your PGA professional you may need to change a position or movement in the swing, and it is sometimes more effective not to make a full swing but to isolate the defect and repeat the correct movement until it starts to blend naturally into the whole swing.

At-home practice drills

It is sometimes difficult to spare enough time to visit a driving range or practice ground, but there are several routines that can be practised easily at home. In fact, in the early stages of learning, these are just as good as hitting the ball although you do need to learn some ball contact and feel as well. Here are some drills for you to try out yourself at home.

Full length mirror drill
Use a mirror to check your set up only. From the front view, check your grip, left arm/club shaft line and ball position; and from the side view, check your posture and alignment.

Putting track drill ▼

Lay a piece of 4 x 2 inch timber flat on the ground. Position the heel of your putter so that it is touching and running along the edge of the wood to give the feeling for the straight section of a correct putting stroke. The length of stroke used would not propel the ball more than about 15 feet on an average-speed surface.

Two club shafts may also be used to give a parallel lines impression to aid the ingraining of a good putting stroke.

One-arm swing

In order to strengthen and gain control, use your left arm only to swing the club, placing your right behind your back and

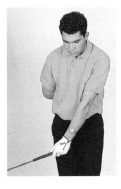 

swinging halfway back and through. Keep your eyes focused on the spot where the ball would be. If you feel that the club is too heavy then move down the grip two or three inches.

Chipping/half swing drill▶

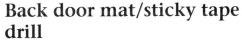

Using airballs or 30 per cent balls, give yourself a target such as a bucket lid into which to chip some balls. Use a mat if necessary to protect your grass.

Back door mat/sticky tape drill

If you have a well-tended lawn from which you don't want to remove any divots, just place your back door mat (coconut type) on some grass or a hard surface outside. You need an object to represent the ball – a piece of tape, a painted mark or some golf tees at which to aim – so that when you swing down to the mat you can see that your club head is returning consistently to the correct point at the bottom of the swing.

Preparing to play

Head against wall drill

Using a towel if wished, stand in your normal set-up position so that your head is lightly touching a wall or door pillar. Adopting your normal golf grip but without a club, your right index finger should be approximately three inches from the wall, and your feet about nine inches away.

The object of the exercise is to feel your head remaining steady whilst your body turns around it. When you swing back and forth notice the arc your hands follow in relation to the wall. They should move away from the wall on both sides and then return close to it in the middle section of the swing (roughly the width of your stance and shoulders). This illustrates perfectly how the golf swing is a circle, on a slant, around your body.

Cross hands resistance exercise

Adopt your proper set-up position and cross your extended arms, with the back of your right hand over and against the back of your left hand. Swing your arms away from the target, turning your body, forcibly resisting with the back of your left hand until you reach the top of the backswing, and then hold for a few seconds. Now from the set-up position again, reverse your hands left over and against right this time. Counter the

Start with the right wrist crossed over the left and the backs of the hands touching. Make a normal backswing turn, forcibly resisting with the back of the left hand.

The hands are now reversed left over right. The follow through movement is made with resistance from the back of the right hand, holding for a few seconds.

swing towards the target by resisting with the back of your right hand and hold the follow-through position for a few seconds. Repeat, concentrating on target side leadership and maintaining consistent balance.

Towel exercise

Hold the centre part of the towel rolled up with your left hand, palm facing down, and your right hand, palm facing up, 12 inches apart. Then adopt your normal stance and posture and swing the towel around your body as if it were a golf club, keeping the towel taut throughout. You should be aware of the rotation of your hands and forearms within the swing. Repeat the exercise with continuous movements.

You can modify the exercise by releasing your right hand just as the forward swing begins, then continuing with the left hand and arm to fling the towel forcefully out towards the target for a high finish.

Place your hands about 12 inches apart, and keep the centre part of the rolled towel taut throughout the swing. Notice how the player's back is turned towards the target in the top photograph. There should be good arm rotation which is beneficial for any golfers who slice to allow the correct golf grip to be used.

Hammer drill

This exercise allows you to practise your swing indoors yet still feel the weight of the club, albeit heavier than a normal club. Whatever you use, make sure that your grip is correct.

The drill uses a heavy hammer. The handle must be roughly the same thickness as that of a golf club to allow the correct golf grip to be used.

Club head control/hands control drill ▶

Keep a club at home in a convenient place to encourage you to pick it up frequently. This allows you to practise your grip and become more familiar with the club as an extension of you. Grip the club and hold the head up at around shoulder height with no bend at your hips. Then trace your name in large letters in the air. Don't move your body or arms, but do this by flexing your hands and wrists up and down and back and forth, all the time looking at the club head.

Remember that your hands are the direct link with the club head – good golf begins with a good grip.

Preparing to play

Long broom drill

Practising with a heavy long object makes you stretch and turn and use your body. Using a very long-handled broom will make you swing on a considerably flatter swing plane so don't overdo this exercise.

Elephant's trunk swing exercise

As a beginner you may find it easier to create a swinging movement without a golf club in your hand. Assume your correct stance and posture, extending your hands in a near-vertical plane and clapping your hands together. Swing your extended arms back and through with a mental picture of both arms swinging together as one, and being initiated from your shoulders. You should use this exercise only at waist height keeping both arms fully extended.

Club support exercises

Take your correct stance and place the palm of your left hand on top of the club shaft which should be vertical. Start with your right hand in a normal grip position but with the fingers pointed downwards so that the palm of your hand faces your imaginary target and your right elbow points inwards towards your right hip.

Then turn your body away to make a backswing letting your right wrist hinge back and keeping your left arm and the club still. Return to the impact position with your hips turned to face the target and your right palm facing the target with some hinge at the wrist retained. Be aware of your right shoulder being lower than your left.

Reverse the exercise with your right hand on top of the club, swinging your left arm back and pulling through with left-side force to a high finishing position. Repeat both these exercises several times.

With the palm of the left hand resting on top of the club shaft, swing the right arm back and return it to a simulated impact position. The hips should start to turn to face the target with the right palm facing slightly downwards.

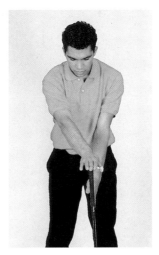

CHAPTER TWO

Building your golf swing

by Jim Christine

So you have made the decision to play the game of golf. I have to say that learning to play golf is difficult, but enormously rewarding, and I hope that in these pages we can help you to enjoy this great game to the full. Your first step is to appreciate what you have to do to play golf successfully; the second is to set about the task of training yourself to move and work in the correct way.

Make no mistake – learning to play golf is a training process, not perhaps as physically demanding as soccer or tennis, but as skilled as playing a musical instrument. It takes time to train your mind to control your muscles in a new way. Many players think that knowing how to move is enough, but unfortunately this is not so – you must practise moves and exercises until they are ingrained and you can repeat these automatically and instinctively.

This chapter will help you to understand what it takes to build a good, consistent golf swing. It is divided into sections, each concentrating on key parts of the golf swing, which when put together will form a simple and cohesive whole.

Each section will outline the technique required, the key learning points, and light exercises which, when repeated, will allow you to teach yourself to swing the club correctly. You should use a mid-iron (ideally a 7, although a 6 or 5 will do) for all the exercises described, as all the original positions referred to are for this type of club.

It is very important that you use good equipment, which is suitable for you, and you should consult your local PGA qualified professional who will make sure that you purchase the best equipment for your build and skills.

On now to the actual game: take your time, practise each part in the correct order, and you will build a game of which you can be proud. Golf is a game of repetition. You will get very little for hitting one good shot every so often! It demands good routine to bring about the consistency of shot required, and that routine starts with the set up.

Building your golf swing

The set up

This is the foundation upon which your ability to take a swing at the ball is based. Preparation of your set up is *very* important: done well, it allows all the subsequent actions to be simple and successful; done badly, it may resign you to never being able to make any progress with your game.

It is all too easy to skim over this first part, rushing on to what many see as the business end of golf – hitting the ball. Please do *not* allow yourself to fall into this trap.

The set up consists of all the things you must do before you take a swing. It separates into five distinct parts, and we will deal with them in the order in which they occur:

1 Aim: align your club to the target;
2 Grip: place your hands on the club;
3 Ball position: position your body in relation to the ball;
4 Body alignment: align your body to the target;
5 Posture: position your body for the shot.

As you deal with these points, it is very important to keep working around your natural body movements, and you will see reference to this throughout the swing-building process.

Aim

The part of the club you aim with is the bottom front edge, called the 'leading edge'. You must establish a right angle (90 degrees) relationship between this edge and your target line in order to aim the club correctly. To do this, prepare your shot in the following way *every* time. This is the beginning of your routine!

Start by standing directly behind your ball, facing your target, looking over the ball towards the target. Establish an imaginary line from the middle of your ball to the middle of your target. This line is called the '**ball-**

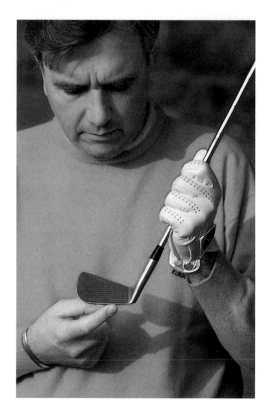

Right: The bottom front edge of your club is called the leading edge.

34

to-target line'. As your target will normally be a reasonable distance away from you, and it will be difficult to keep a good fix on it as you move to take up your position at the ball, you will find it helps to pick out something on your ball-to-target line to aim your shot over. This is called your 'forward marker' – it could be a leaf, an old divot, a twig or a broken tee – anything you can see clearly. You will find it much easier to aim over your forward marker two to three yards away than towards a target 200 yards in the distance.

You should now find it reasonably easy to walk towards your ball and place the leading edge of your club at 90 degrees to your ball-to-target line. You have now achieved the correct aim.

Key learning points

You should now understand:
● Leading edge of the club face.
● Ball-to-target line.
● That the correct aim of the club is when you establish a 90 degrees relationship between the leading edge and the ball-to-target line.

Right: Using a forward marker aim your club correctly at your intended target.

Building your golf swing

The grip

This is your connection to the golf club, your only means of establishing and maintaining control over it. The grip is therefore a vital area of your game.

The word grip is used to describe the **position** of the hands, not the strength with which you grasp the club. The term can therefore be misleading. Do not get the idea of vice-like strength, as some people do, from the word grip. Think of it rather as a *hold*, and you will have more of an idea of the feeling and strength of grasp.

The grip is the first example that illustrates how the natural positions of the body are an integral part of the golf swing. If you were going to slap something with either of your hands you would attempt to do so with your hand flat and square as it comes into contact with the object. This concept is the basis of holding the club correctly – a golf club is just an extension of your hands and arms; whatever your hands do will be reflected and extended by the club.

Let's explore this more deeply: think of the following example and you will understand the essential, and very simple, principles of a good grip. Imagine hitting something with your hand, then with something small such as a table tennis bat, then with something larger such as a tennis racket, and finally a golf club. The principles of controlling the blade of a table tennis bat, the head of a tennis racket and the leading edge of a golf club are one and

Above: Position the club at right angles to your body.

Right: Place your left hand in a shake hands position.

Lay the club diagonally through the left hand from the second joint of your index finger to a point just above the base of your little finger.

36

the same. The head of the club which you are trying to control is further away from you, but nothing else is different – you are standing to the side of the ball, trying to hit it forward along a desired line.

Once you have this principle in mind, it is easy to see that you must introduce your hands to the club in their natural 'shake-hands' position. There must be no rotation in your fore-arms or hands before you start to position them on the club.

Take your grip in the following order:

1 Take the club in the thumb and fore-finger of your right hand and aim the club face at a right angle to your ball-to-target line and your body.

2 Place your left hand beside the grip in the 'shake-hands' position with your fingers pointing at the ground.

3 Rest the club on the second joint of your left index finger and let it run diagonally across your hand to a point in your palm just above the base of your little finger.

4 Close your hand around the grip and you will find that your left thumb comes to rest just to the right of the centre of the grip and the heel of your hand rests on the top of the grip.

5 Now check the correct position of your left hand – the 'V' between your thumb and forefinger should be pointing midway between your chin and right shoulder. You should be able to see two knuckles on the back of your left hand.

6 Now place your right hand on the club, again starting with the natural 'shake-hands' position. Rest the club on the bottom joints of your two middle fingers and the middle joint of your index finger which must be 'triggered' to make this possible. The little finger of

Check the completed left hand grip for position.

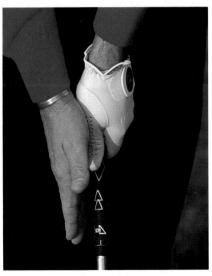

Place your right hand in a shake hands position.

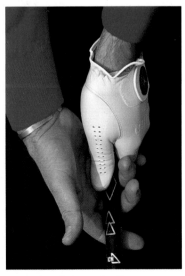

Rest the club on the bottom two joints of your middle two fingers.

Building your golf swing

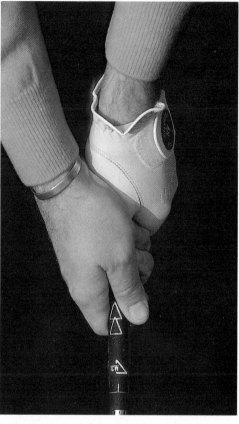

Right: Check the established grip for position.

Far right: This is the overlap of the left little finger onto the right hand.

should point to the same place as the 'V' formed between the thumb and fore-finger of your left hand.

You have now positioned your hands on the club in the correct way – this means that your grip will allow you to make a proper swing.

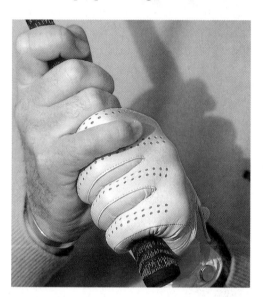

your right hand should rest on top of the index finger of your left hand.

7 Close your hand around the grip – you will find your right thumb coming to rest just to the left of the centre of the grip, and the 'V' formed between the thumb and forefinger of your right hand

Key learning points

● The aim of the grip is to establish the placing of your hands on the club by the method discussed.
● You should also achieve a good degree of comfort in the correct holding position.

Practice

Go through the procedure des-cribed from start to finish, waggle the club around a little, take your hands off the club, and go through the whole procedure again. Repeat this five times, remembering the waggle at the end, and on finishing the fifth time have a rest. Do this two or three times a day and in no time you will become accustomed to the position your hands should adopt on the club.

Ball position

The ball must be positioned in the forward half of the stance (halfway between the centre of your feet and your front foot) for all normal shots. This makes the back of the ball available for you to strike, and places you in a position where you will be encouraged to use your body weight correctly through the swing.

A good method of establishing the ball position is to stand with your feet together (far left). Move your left foot into the correct position in relation to the ball (bottom left), then establish the stance width by moving your right foot (left).

Building your golf swing

Body alignment

This is positioning your body in relation to your **target**. You should align your toes, knees, hips and shoulders parallel to the ball-to-target line. This ensures that your swing will direct the ball towards the target.

Practice

Place two clubs on the ground, one running parallel to your ball-to-target line and one at right angles to it. They should make the shape of a capital letter 'T', and there should be a gap of about 12 inches between them.

Face the shaft, which is running parallel with your ball-to-target line, making sure that your toes, knees, hips and shoulders are parallel to it. Use the other shaft running back between your feet to indicate the position of the ball, and make sure that this is halfway between the centre of your feet and your left foot. This is the ideal position for a medium iron.

Right: It is very important to position your shoulders parallel to the ball to target line, so it makes sense to keep your toes, knees and hips parallel too. You will find any lines placed on the ground parallel to your target line a great help during practice.

Posture

This is the positioning of your body at set up, and good posture will establish:

1 A stable, balanced position from which you can move freely.

2 The correct distance between you and the ball.

3 The correct angle of swing to produce a solid strike on the back of the ball.

The golf swing is an athletic movement involving practically every part of your body. The posture position is the final link in your set up and must place you in readiness for that free athletic movement.

Key learning points

You need good posture to ensure that you:

● Establish a position that will give you the opportunity to move freely and to remain balanced during your swing.

● Establish the correct distance between you and the ball.

● Establish the correct angle of swing.

Right: Good posture is the key to balanced, athletic movement.

Building your golf swing

Practice

This drill will give you the opportunity to practise your posture in harmony with everything you have learned so far.

Place two clubs on the ground as you did for ball position and body alignment. There is no need to use a ball; in fact, it is much better not to at this stage. One club shows the parallel line to your ball-to-target line, and the other where the ball is in relation to your feet.

Make sure that the leading edge

Set the angle of your feet so that your left toes point to 11 o'clock on an imaginary clockface and your right to 1 o'clock. Adjust your position until the club shaft between your feet is midway between the centre of your stance and your left heel.

Look straight ahead at your own height, and extend your arms and club in front of you until the shaft is parallel with the ground at waist level. Lean forwards from your hips until the bottom of the club rests

Top right: Don't stretch or get too close (bottom right). Establish your natural hitting distance (far right).

of your club face is in the correct position and take up your grip. Move forward to the clubs on the ground and stand facing the club indicating the parallel line to your target. Make sure that your toes, knees, hips and shoulders are parallel to it. Place your feet apart so that a line drawn down from the inside of each of your arms runs through the middle of each foot.

lightly on the ground. If you do this correctly, you should feel the hamstrings in the back of each of your legs becoming tighter. Take this tightness away by lightly flexing your knees. You should have a lively, bouncy feeling in your body which shows you are ready for physical activity – ready to move the club freely into a good golf swing. Your weight should be distributed evenly between the balls and heels of each foot, and, with the mid-iron you are using, it should also be distributed evenly between your left and right foot. Your hands should be opposite the inside of your left thigh and four to five inches from it. Your chin should still be clear of your chest, and by looking down with your eyes, you should be able to see clearly the club head on the ground. The club face will be parallel to the line between your feet, and eventually you will learn to position the ball in front of the centre of the club face. Hence this

drill will show you where the ball should lie so that you can strike it correctly during your swing.

Waggle the club a little and change your weight distribution from foot to foot, finally returning to the correct position. This will help you to prevent any tension developing in your set up. Repeat this exercise five times. It will teach you:

1 The correct posture at set up to achieve the correct weight distribution, spine angle and distance from the ball for the club you are using.

2 How to practise using your entire set up routine.

Far left: Bend forward from your hips until the club touches the ground and then flex your knees (left).

Building your golf swing

Swinging the club

Having now established the correct set up, you are ready to swing. The purpose of your swing is to generate power. Generating power is the only reason for taking a swing, but in that short statement lies the biggest danger to all golfers! Most golfers, especially new, untrained golfers, hurl themselves around so much in an attempt to generate power that they have little chance of hitting the ball properly, far less sending it in the correct direction.

This is quite natural. When you stand on a teeing ground and look down the fairway, what is the first thing forced into a new golfer's mind? How far away the flag seems! The next question is, "How do I manage to hit the ball that far?" "Hit it hard" seems a reasonable answer for most beginners.

Hence without the proper training it is very easy for a new golfer to fall into the habit of trying to hit the ball much too hard. This means that it will be very difficult to control any of the actions you are trying to make. Power has taken over and accuracy and control could well be lost for ever. If you imagine on your first driving lesson that you are told to drive the car as fast as you can round an obstacle course, you would have a good comparison with learning to play golf in the way I have described above. Do not let this happen to you.

It is important to remember that you will achieve far more distance from a ball struck well with less power than from a ball struck badly and with more power. Take your time, and read through these pages in order! Never force a shot in an attempt just to hit it further. *Think of hitting the ball better, not harder!*

To swing the club well means that you will generate power whilst giving yourself a reasonable opportunity to strike the ball accurately and send it in the correct direction. This demands a well balanced, co-ordinated movement marrying together the two areas of power generation: your body action, and the areas you will be working on firstly to understand them and then train yourself to put them into practice.

The body action
As it contains the strongest muscles in your golf swing, it is vital to use your body correctly. It is the biggest source of power in the swing and how it moves will also determine how well you are able to swing your arms, hands and club. How you use your body will be responsible for:
● The ability to use your large muscles correctly.
● The amount of power you generate.
● The ability of your arms, hands and club to achieve the correct swing.
● The overall pace of your golf swing.

The body action has to achieve a good pivoting motion as well as the correct weight transfer during your swing. The pivoting action will be largely responsible for your ability to return the club head consistently and accurately to the ball. It will also join together with your weight transfer to generate the power you require to send the ball the distance needed to play the game successfully.

Your body is going to pivot and move your weight into your right side during the backswing.From there it can be used to help strike the ball forward as your body pivots into and then around your left side taking your weight all the way through on to your left foot by the end of your swing. Let's see how you are going to train yourself to do this.

The backswing pivot

The pivot starts with your body beginning to turn, transferring weight on to your right foot. As you continue turning, your weight moves more and more into your right side. You must keep the flex in your right knee constant throughout the movement in order to make sure that your weight stays directly above your right foot and does not move over on to the outside of this foot.

At the end of this movement your shoulders should have turned a little beyond 90 degrees from their original position. Your hips should have turned between 30 and 40 degrees, depending on how supple you are, and 75 per cent of your body weight should be over your right foot.

You must not try to keep your head too still during this movement, as this will only serve to encourage you not to transfer your weight or to turn incorrectly, resulting in a very restricted position. Allow it to turn a little to the right

– your swing will be all the better for it.

You have now completed your backswing. At the end of the backswing, you should feel a little tension in your right thigh and across the left side of your back. This is an indication of the power you have stored up ready to use when striking the ball.

The downswing

The downswing begins by moving the whole of your left side smoothly across until you find that 50 per cent of your weight is on your left foot. You should then begin to turn your upper left side behind you, bringing more of your

A technically sound swing requires the body pivot and the arm swing to work in complete harmony.

Building your golf swing

weight on to your left foot as this movement continues. Your right side should be pulled through by the movement of your left until, at the end of the swing, your shoulders have turned to the point where your right shoulder is closer to the target than your left, your hips are at 90 degrees to the ball-to-target line, and 90 per cent of your weight is over your left foot with only the toe of your right foot resting on the ground.

Your head must be allowed to move through this movement, finishing in a position where you can look down the target line. Throughout the entire movement the angle of your spine, created by your posture at set up, should remain constant.

Key learning points

During the swing your body action should:
● Maintain balance throughout the swing.
● Maintain spinal angle throughout the swing.
● Control weight transfer.
● Create controlled power.
● Control the speed of the swing.

Practice

As this pivoting motion is really quite difficult to learn, you may find it easier to practise first in an upright position rather than your usual golfing position.

Start with a club held across your shoulders as shown in the photograph. As your spine is upright, the pivot you are going to practise will be horizontal. Move your right side slowly, turning it behind you, and check that your weight is already beginning to transfer to your right foot. Continue moving until you feel that you have turned your shoulders through 90 degrees. (You may find it helpful to do this drill in front of a mirror so that you can easily appreciate how far you are moving.)

At the end of your backswing, 75 per cent of your weight should be on your right foot and you should feel a little tension in your right thigh and across the left side of your back. If you do not feel this tension, check your right knee position – it will probably be straight and your hips will have turned more than 45 degrees. If you flex your right knee a little, the amount of your hip turn should reduce, and you will feel the tension in the correct places. (If this proves a problem for you, practise retaining the flex in your right knee as you continue to use this drill.)

Begin the movement back into the downswing with the whole of your left side. You should feel the pivot smoothly moving your weight on to your left foot, returning close, but not quite, to your original set up position. You are now in the area of the swing where you would be nearing the striking position, and your body should reflect this. You must feel dynamic, and therefore there should be a little more weight on your left foot than on your right. Your upper left side should now begin pivoting to the left, moving behind you, just as the right side did in the backswing. Keep the movement at a slow pace and feel more of your weight moving on to your left foot as you continue to turn. Carry on all the way through until you reach the finishing position.

You should be well balanced throughout the exercise and you should repeat these movements until you feel comfortable with them.

This upright pivoting exercise allows you to develop the feel of the golf swing body action from a natural position. Concentrate on a good 90 degrees pivot back and through, and establish control of your weight transfer and balance.

Building your golf swing

Practice

Now that you feel that you have achieved a good degree of control in this upright position, repeat the exercise beginning in your golf posture position. It is again a great help to work initially in front of a mirror, as you must make sure that you are retaining the angle of your spine throughout the movement and that your shoulders stay in a 90 degrees relationship to your spine.

Do not rush; there is no hurry. This is the foundation of your swing, and one correct, slow exercise is better than any number of fast incorrect ones.

Use your pivoting exercise from your correct posture position now. Check your movement in a mirror, watching closely the angle of your spine. The angle you establish at set up must remain constant throughout the exercise.

Building your golf swing

The arm swing

This the area of the swing concerning your arms, hands and club. These have to be related correctly to your body action if you are going to be able to stand any chance of returning the club to the ball correctly and consistently. You must use the leverage supplied by your arms and hands to build up power, but this has to be done in a way that gives you the best possible chance of returning the club accurately to the ball.

The swing plane

At this stage you must be introduced to the concept of 'swing plane' because understanding this and then training yourself to comply with it is your next step forward.

The plane of a golf swing is the angle in which the club moves as it is swung around the body. The correct swing plane is established at set up by assuming the correct posture, and is defined as the angle of an imaginary line drawn from your throat to the ball and the ground.

This is the angle that you will establish and maintain with your arm swing, and, having done so, you will have the consistency required to play well on a regular basis.

At the beginning of the movement, everything should move together, maintaining the relationship you established at set up. This lasts until your hands reach a point above your right shoe. At this stage, your right arm will begin to soften at the elbow and your right wrist will begin to set. As the motion continues, your arms, hands and club will be established in the swing plane as they reach waist level, and as you move further, the shaft should move on to the swing plane angle. At the end of the backswing, your left arm will be comfortably straight, and your right elbow will be in a fully folded position with the elbow pointing towards the ground, just behind your heels. The bottom front edge of the club should be parallel to the plane of your swing.

The downswing

During the downswing, the relationship created between your arms, hands and club is maintained until you reach the delivery position. These moves are really a reaction to your body action at this stage of the swing and should not require any conscious thought. You will

Key points

- There should be no independent movement in your arms and hands.
- The plane of the swing is the key to correct and consistent striking of the ball.
- Your arms and hands should keep moving on the swing plane.

50

however practise this in your arm swing drill. From here you will release the angles in your right arm smoothly, thus delivering a strong, square hit at the back of the ball. Momentum should now carry your arms through, with your body action taking them into a full finish position. The shaft will lie across the back of your head, your right arm should be comfortably straight, and your left upper arm should be in line with your shoulders.

Practice

Take up the position shown in front of a mirror; this will help you to appreciate how you are moving. This is a slight modification of your normal set up position and is achieved by taking your grip on the shaft of the club just below the bottom of the grip. The butt end of the club should rest on your body approximately where your belt buckle would be if you were wearing a belt.

As you make your takeaway, it will be obvious if there is any independent movement, as either:

1 You will feel the club pressing into your body or;

2 the butt of the club will move away from your body.

Having reached the end of your takeaway in one piece, your right arm will now bring the club away from your body so that, at waist height, the shaft will be parallel to both your ball-to-target line and the ground. The leading edge of your club will be in a vertical position.

As the right arm continues to fold at the elbow, and the wrist sets, you will see the shaft come into plane angle at the three-quarters swing position. Your right wrist should now be fully set, and at this stage, the arms and hands have finished their work. Achieving the top of the backswing is just a matter of completing your body action.

As your body moves your weight back into your left side, your arms, hands and club are pulled into the delivery position where once again

This exercise position is a modification of your set up position. Slide the club up through your hands until it rests on your body just where your belt buckle would be.

Building your golf swing

practice continued . . .

the shaft is parallel with both your ball-to-target line and the ground. Once again, the leading edge of your club should be held vertically.

Your upper left side now begins to pivot around behind you allowing the free, square release of the club into the back of the ball, and you will simulate this by repositioning the butt of your club against your body. This time, because of the athletic position of your body, the point at which you should place the club against your body will be a couple of inches to the left of your imaginary belt buckle – still, however, on the belt itself. Make sure that your club is back at 90 degrees to your ball-to-target line.

Keep the contact against your body until your hands pass over your left shoe, when you should allow your left arm to begin to fold and set as your right did in the backswing.

As the club reaches waist level, once again the shaft will lie both parallel to your ball-to-target line and the ground, with the leading edge vertical. Your right arm should be comfortably straight.

Continue this folding and setting of your left arm until the shaft once again lies in the plane angle at the three-quarters through position.

Moving on to the finish of the swing, the shaft should lie across the back of your head at an angle a little shallower than the swing plane resulting from the straightening of your spinal angle in the later stages of the movement. Your upper left arm will be in line with your shoulders

and your right arm will be comfortably straight.

Although this is an exercise to help you learn to position your arms, hands and club correctly through the swing, it does demand that your body action works correctly before it can be of any valid use in your training programme. *You must be able to rely on your body action working correctly before you should even begin your arm swing training.*

Building your golf swing

A practice session

You have now developed the movements required to make a good golf swing. However, the next question is will it make contact with the ball? It is

Above: After a few easy practice swings towards the ground, just letting the club brush across the grass, use a tee peg as your first object to strike.

now time to begin to learn how to use the movements you have learned to actually play the game.

To start with, your practice exercises will still not involve using a ball; this will follow after a few minutes. When this time comes, tee the ball up on a short plastic tee and make sure that the bottom of the ball is just above the level of the grass. This will give you a little extra help to hit a good shot at the beginning.

However, let us not get ahead of ourselves! The first few swings you take in earnest will be at a much bigger target – Mother Earth. If you make contact with the ground, you should be happy! You are going to start by learning to feel the weight of the club. Swing back as far as your three-quarters position, swing

smoothly through to a finish and see if you brush the grass. Check your balance – you must maintain control. Try to feel the weight of the club acting under

gravity, stay relaxed and the club head should just brush across the grass. Tension will be your big problem, but if you keep repeating the three-quarters

54

swing you will begin to feel more accustomed to the movement. The more confident you feel, the more relaxed you will become, and brushing the grass will seem too easy.

Now put a tee in the way as described above. Go through the same exercise, stay relaxed, and you will brush the tee out of the grass. Do not make a hit at it – just work through your swing movement, and the tee should get in the way.

Well, sooner or later, the ball had to appear on the scene! Now pop one on to the top of your tee. Do not worry too much about an exact aim – just try to aim down the centre of the area at which you are hitting. Again, keep your swing smooth and do not try to smack the ball hard – just let it get in the way.

Keep your first swings at a nice three-quarter length. Feel the weight of the club swinging towards the grass.

Building your golf swing

You will find the club's loft will put the ball in the air, and you will have hit your first real golf shot. Well done!

Keep repeating your swing, using plenty of practice swings as well as

On to the ball now. Stay relaxed and allow the movements you have developed to work automatically. Do not force the shot. Let the ball get in the way of the club and that great swing!

hitting the ball, until you feel confident with your three-quarters swing. Ease through to a full swing position and you will find that the ball will travel a little further. As your confidence grows, you will move faster and the ball will go further. Let your balance be your guide and *never* lose it – if you do, you are putting in too much effort.

Having gone through this process, you now want to aim at a specific target. You have got over the first hurdle of playing some proper shots, and now you must make sure that you can play them in the correct direction. You must not

do this too early in your practice session as it will make you try too hard; the result will be tension, and you will not hit any good shots.

Repeat the shots with your full swing, making sure that you pick a target to aim at. Find a forward marker, and go through the whole routine to establish the correct aim. Once posi-

Building your golf swing

tioned, play the shot freely. Remember that the swing is for striking the ball and you should not be conscious of trying to guide it to the target. A good swing, aimed correctly, will let the ball go down the correct line automatically.

If you are having real success, try hitting a few shots without a tee. Find a good high spot on the grass or a nice even piece of practice mat, and keep everything the same, sticking to your routine, making a relaxed swing and

seeing what happens.

Do not worry if there does not seem to be much in the way of success. Learning to play golf takes time. Keep on with your training exercises, give yourself a few practice sessions, and everything will fit into place eventually. *Always* begin a practice session with some practice swings. Eventually you will dispense with swings at a tee peg, but take your time building up your shots. Do not play more than two balls

per minute, even fewer ideally. Also never let your practice sessions go on for too long. Thirty to forty five minutes is a good length of time to spend.

It is essential to make sure that you always continue with your training exercises. These are the moves that form and improve your golf swing. It is advisable to spend more time on the exercises without the ball than hitting shots. Only then will your technique advance into a good, sound golf swing.

This sequence shows the moment of impact and a good follow through. At the finish of the swing, the shaft should lie across the back of your head at a slightly shallower angle than the swing plane. Your right arm should be comfortably straight and your upper left arm should be in line with your shoulders.

Building your golf swing

Other clubs

Having learned to swing a mid-iron using all the information and exercises above, you need to understand a little more to help you to use your other clubs. You have to learn slight adjustments to your weight distribution, width of stance and ball position when using different clubs. Other adjustments in your set up and swing will follow automatically from these. The only conscious changes you need to make are the ones outlined here; the rest will take place as you follow your normal routine.

Golf clubs split into three groups:
1 The mid-irons: 5, 6 and 7, which you already know.
2 The woods and long irons.
3 The short irons.

The 'woods and long irons' consist of all the woods and the 1, 2, 3 and 4 irons; the 'short irons' consist of the 8, 9, pitching wedge and sand iron.

At this stage of your golfing career, please do not even think of using a 1 or 2 wood or a 1 or 2 iron. These are the most difficult clubs to use and must be saved for a later date.

Short irons
These clubs are designed to give the ball a reasonably high floating style of flight which will stop the ball quickly on the green. Due to their short shaft, they will not send the ball as far as your mid-irons, thereby giving you the ability to play shorter shots.

For a short iron, reduce the width of your stance so that a line drawn down from the inside of each arm extends to the outside of each foot. This gives the correct amount of stability and mobility for these shots. You should feel slightly more weight on your left foot – try to achieve a weight distribution of 55 per cent on your left foot and 45 per cent on your right. This will give you the correct angle of swing for these clubs.

The rest of your routine remains the same: aim, grip, ball position and body alignment. These small adjustments in width of stance and weight distribution are all that are necessary. Having done these, follow through your posture routine and swing as normal for a successful short iron shot.

Right: The short irons need a narrower stance so that you can stay mobile during this less dynamic area of the game.

Left: The correct stance width for your medium irons. Place your feet so that the middle of each foot is directly under the inside of each arm.

Building your golf swing

Right: Keep using your practice drill with clubs or lines on the ground to help you position yourself correctly. Here I am checking the ball position and stance alignment for a fairway wood.

Woods and long irons

These clubs are designed to send the ball further while you keep your swing the same. Do not fall into the trap of forcing these shots – use the procedures described below to accommodate the club you are using, and swing as you have already learned.

The clubs you are now using have longer shafts and therefore are the exact opposite to your short irons. They create more momentum and hence require a more stable stance than your mid-irons; otherwise there will be a danger of falling off balance. The length of shaft also means that the arc of your swing will be a little shallower and this makes a more sweeping type of strike desirable.

To accommodate these requirements, you will need to widen your stance a little and move the ball position in your stance. This will change your weight distribution at set up.

Place your feet apart so that a line drawn down from the inside of each arm will extend to the inside of each foot. Now position the ball opposite the inside of your left heel.

These two changes will make your weight distribution 55 per cent on your right foot and 45 per cent on your left.

Once again follow through your normal set up routine and practise this slightly different position. Use your full set up drill described at the end of the posture section, and you will soon become accustomed to the small changes of set up required to accommodate these longer clubs.

Summary

This chapter has taken you through the very fundamentals of building a good, consistent golf swing. As said in the introduction, learning to play golf is a training process, demanding time to train your mind to control your muscles in a new way. Much of this process may seem a little laborious at first, but taking each step at a time and doing the practice exercises for each individual part of the swing, will ensure that you build a good swing which will last you until well into old age.

Left: Your longer clubs develop more momentum, and therefore a slightly wider stance is necessary to maintain your stability.

CHAPTER THREE

The Long Game

by Nigel Blenkarne

A well hit long and straight shot using a wood or long iron will always give you great satisfaction. However, it is essential that you learn and incorporate the fundamentals that make up a consistent and reliable method, starting with the all-important set up, grip, stance. posture and aim.

You are not required to learn a different swing for each club – the basics remain the same. The only changes you must make are the distance you stand from the ball and the positioning of the ball in your stance to accommodate the length and design of each club. You must accept that the longer shafted, straighter faced clubs are more difficult to control and hit consistently well. Therefore, it is wise to start out with the middle clubs and progress to the longer ones gradually.

The natural tendency with a long club is to swing too hard in an effort to hit the ball a long way. In fact, because the shaft is longer and the club head is travelling on a bigger arc, the very opposite is necessary: a slower swing. The best advice for your long game is: *don't force it*, make a smooth unhurried swing.

Judging distance

The purpose of judging distance is to help you select the correct club to hit the ball to the target. Your first priority in this task is to know within 10 yards how far you hit each club, given a good connection. When you start in golf you must expect mishit shots that do not reach your target, but you should always select your club in the hope that you will hit a good shot.

Opposite: Payne Stewart tees off with St Andrews in the background. Judging distance is very important in the long game, and in this photograph the green appears closer than it is in reality.

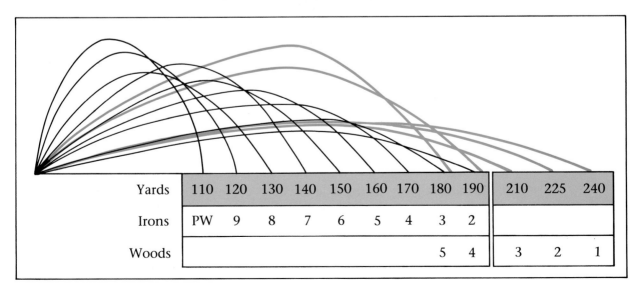

Yards	110	120	130	140	150	160	170	180	190		210	225	240
Irons	PW	9	8	7	6	5	4	3	2				
Woods								5	4		3	2	1

The long game

On a calm, warm day go to a level practice ground with about 20 balls. (They should all be the same make – preferably the type you use when playing.) Hit all 20 balls with one middle club (a 6 or 7 iron) and then pace out to the centre of the group of good shots, trying to make your strides a yard each in length. You can then estimate fairly accurately how far each iron club will go; between each club there will be approximately 10 yards. For example, if your well-hit 6 iron goes 150 yards, a 7 iron should go 140 yards, and a 5 iron 160 yards. It is your iron clubs that you rely on as the accuracy approach clubs, with the woods being the distance clubs which you should expect to have a greater differential, nearer 20 yards between clubs. Following on from this example you would expect to achieve the distances shown in the chart.

Course plans – yardage charts

The majority of golf courses now have a pre-measured course planner which tells you the distance you have to the centre or front of the green (always check this measurement). Fifteen years ago they did not exist and every shot had to be judged by eye.

Break yardage down into sections

By standing slightly to the side of the shot you have to play, you can judge the distance that remains better than if you were standing behind the ball. Then split the distance into two or three so that you can see a 50-yard mark, followed by another 50-yard mark and you can add these to gauge a more accurate picture rather than looking purely from the ball straight at the target.

There are a number of factors that need to be considered before finally selecting the right club for the shot. These are as follows:

● Wind direction and strength (especially on exposed courses).
● Temperature – a warm ball travels up to 20 yards further than a cold ball.
● Ground firmness – will the ball stop quickly or run, and if so how much?
● A backdrop of trees or a bank behind the green tends to make it look closer than it is.
● No background behind the green tends to give the impression that it is further than it is.
● The size of the greens – large greens look closer whereas small greens look further away than they actually are.
● The length of the flagsticks have a similar visual effect – long ones look closer whereas short ones look further away.
● Be aware that there may be 'dead ground' especially if you are playing over mounds.

It will really pay dividends and help your scores if you work on knowing the distance you hit each club and correctly selecting the right number iron or wood for each shot. A variation or misjudgement in distance by, for example, 30 yards can be just as destructive as hitting a shot 30 yards off line. So don't waste good shots by incorrect club selection.

Fairway woods – 3, 4 and 5 woods

Traditionally the fairway woods consisted of numbers 3 and 4 but in modern times they have expanded to include numbers 5, 7 and 9 woods. The main reason for the more lofted fairway woods increasing in popularity is that many golfers find them easier to use than the long straighter-faced iron clubs. Look at the table which shows you the average lofts on the club faces of different fairway woods or metal headed woods.

The nature of the design of a fairway wood requires you to sit the wide sole of the club flat on the ground

Above right: The sole of the wood is sitting flat in the correct position. Notice the angle of the shaft. Right: The incorrect way to ground a wood. The back edge is up and the loft on the face has been reduced to zero.

Below: This table shows the average lofts on the club faces of fairway woods or metal headed woods, with the equivalent distances using irons.

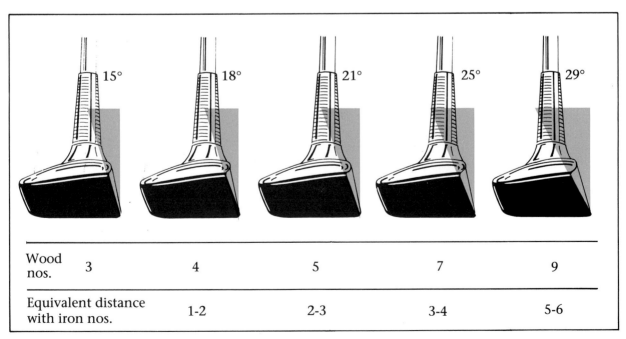

	15°	18°	21°	25°	29°
Wood nos.	3	4	5	7	9
Equivalent distance with iron nos.		1-2	2-3	3-4	5-6

The long game

The distance from the ball varies to accommodate the length of shaft. Here we see the 3 wood, 3 iron and 9 iron. Notice that your posture and arm position in relation to the body do not change.

with the ball positioned opposite your left heel. Therefore, your hands will be level or just slightly behind the back of the ball. It is this factor, combined with the long shaft of a wood club, which helps you to produce a sweeping arc of contact on the ball, as opposed to the more downward contact you get with an iron club.

To check the correct set-up position, ground your fairway wood on a hard flat surface with the club face aimed down the target line. Notice the angle at which the shaft is pointing. (Don't grip the club but just hold it lightly in the fingers of one hand.) Then build your stance around the club and take your grip. Wind conditions should be considered before selecting a fairway wood as opposed to a long iron.

A 5 wood, for example, will tend to flight the ball on a higher trajectory than a 2 or a 3 iron. Therefore when playing into a strong wind, play a long iron as you don't want the ball too high in the air.

For this reason the learner golfer, who will find it more difficult to get the ball flighted, finds it easier to use the lofted fairway woods.

Right: In the set up for fairway woods the ball is positioned opposite the left heel, and the hands are level with the back of the ball.

The long game

In semi-rough, where the grass is longer, a fairway wood-shaped club will tend to sweep through the grass whereas the grass may grab and twist a long iron club. However, be cautious if the ball is sitting down really low as it may be too ambitious to try and hit any long club, and the safe percentage shot would be a lofted short iron club.

Remember that you must be able to strike the ball below its equator to consider using a wood. To use a 3 wood from the fairway you will need a good lie with the whole of the ball sitting above the turf.

Right: A grassy lie just off the fairway is safe to use a wood provided that you can set the club to contact below the ball's equator.

Medium irons – 5, 6 and 7 irons

These are your target clubs. Primarily they are your accuracy clubs used to approach the green from 130 - 170 yards away on average. Never hit the ball flat out with a medium iron; there are no prizes for using the shortest club possible. Most amateur golfers under-club, and even a well-struck shot struggles to reach the front of the green. The depth of the green will probably measure 30-35 yards, giving you two or three clubs difference in aiming to hit the front or back of the green.

Try to assess the pin position and whether more trouble is in front of or behind the green before making your final choice of club, which will often fall among the medium iron group.

Set up

The ball should be positioned three to four inches inside your left heel with your hands slightly forward of the ball so that the club shaft forms an extension line from your left arm (when looking from front view, not side view).

Above: The grip for medium irons with the hands positioned normally with 1½ inches showing at the top of the grip.
Right: In the set up for the 5 iron, the ball is 3-4 inches inside the left heel and the left arm and club shaft are in line.

The long game

Bad lies

In addition, the medium irons are useful for playing back on to the fairway from bad lies if you hit an off-line tee shot. The 7 iron is a particularly good club to use when the ball is down in thick rough and only the top is visible, because the shorter shaft gives a steeper swing, and there is sufficient loft to get the ball airborne with some forward movement.

Above: A bad lie. There is too much grass between the club face and the ball to attempt a long iron or a wood. Use a middle to short club – a 6 iron being the maximum in this instance.

Playing in the wind

It is far easier to use the wind than to fight it. For example, if playing into a left-to-right wind, do not try and draw the shot. Simply set yourself up to allow for the wind and play a normal straight shot which the wind will move back onto the target. You need to visualize the target – in this case, left of its actual position – and then swing towards your imagined target.

When playing into or across the wind, use a larger club than normal, swing a little shorter and **don't force it**. A wider stance will help you to maintain balance and tends to restrict the amount of body turn and therefore the length of the swing. Use the same principles as when playing a low shot. To judge the wind direction:

- Look at the flag.
- Look at the tree tops.
- Hold a handkerchief up.

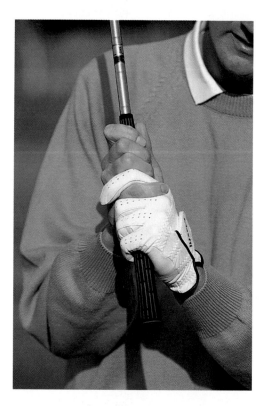

Above: When playing into the wind you should choke down the grip, leaving 3-4 inches showing at the top. This should also be used for playing low punch shots, half shots and recoveries from trees.

The set up for a low medium iron into the wind. Position the ball just behind the centre of the stance with the hands forward. Note the shaft angle.

CHAPTER FOUR

Hazards
by Nigel Blenkarne

When referring to hazards it is important to establish what a hazard is in terms of understanding and applying the Rules of Golf. You are not permitted to ground your club or touch anything in the hazard before hitting the shot.

Whilst there are many situations on a golf course that are hazardous, the only areas that are classified as hazards are water and sand. We should refer to other positions as obstacles to be negotiated; these parts of the course are classed as through the green. So trees, rough, uneven lies, grass hollows and banks are not hazards but they are included in this chapter because on many occasions you will find yourself faced with a shot that requires some variation to your normal swing in order to recover from an awkward position.

Once you realise the changes you need to make in your address and swing to play these shots from hazards and to avoid obstacles, they become less fearsome. However, do not be too ambitious; you should try these shots on a practice ground or by playing the course on your own when you should drop the ball in awkward places. You must be confident that you are capable of pulling off a recovery shot. That confidence will come only by experiencing the successful execution of the shot.

The rough

The first point to establish is whether the severity of the lie prevents you from playing a club long enough to reach the green. If it does, then don't take any risks; take a lofted club and play out to the middle of the fairway.

Novice golfers will often hit their ball into trouble and then try for a miracle recovery shot which may come off one in ten times, but the other nine times will end up in worse trouble. It is in this area of the game that the accomplished player has learned when to take a calculated risk and when to play safe.

Depending on the texture of the rough it will influence the club head in a number of ways as you swing through it. The main consideration is that there will be more resistance and a tendency to twist as the club head contacts the rough and the ball. Your grip must be made **firmer** to allow for this, especially in the top three fingers of your left hand.

Due to the rough grabbing the hosel (heel) of the club, it is usual to expect the club face to close in impact, thereby causing the ball to fly left of the point at which you are aiming. You should simply aim 10-15 yards right of your target with both the club face and your feet and then, during the swing, try to forget that you allowed for this.

Your club face will not make direct contact with the ball when playing from the rough, and there will be a certain

Above: The ball is sitting down, or plugged, making direct club to ball contact impossible. Take a lofted club and hit down into the ground and the ball.

Hazards

amount of grass trapped between the two. This causes the ball to react differently, and it will tend to fly lower and shoot forwards with no backspin on landing, and therefore you must allow for this.

It is advisable to select a more lofted club, play the ball further towards your right foot, and produce a steeper downward angle of attack on the ball. You will be asking for trouble if you try and use a straight-faced club when playing from heavy rough.

Ball sitting up high in the rough

Occasionally, the ball will sit up high on top of the rough and may be two or three inches from the hard ground. You must be careful to:

1 Not ground your club too hard in address (and risk moving the ball).
2 Not to hit under the ball taking the grass beneath it.

Hold the club head so that you are addressing level with the middle of the ball and produce a sweeping action. You must avoid a steep downward strike if the ball is sitting up.

Heather always presents a deceptive problem and is very tough and wiry to play from. Do not be tempted to try any kind of long shot; take your penalty and play a 9 iron or wedge to move the ball forward 60 or 70 yards back on to the fairway.

Above: When the ball is sitting up, do not press the club head down into the ground. Right: When playing from heather, you should use a lofted club and a firm grip.

Bunker play

Mention the word bunker to most beginners and high-handicap golfers and you register instant fear. However, there is no need to worry for once you have grasped the basic technique, extracting your ball from a bunker need not be difficult. Judging distance and precise accuracy take time and practice but your priority is to get out every time in one shot!

Recognise first that this shot requires a different technique to any standard grass lie on the golf course. For a start, it is the only shot in which you should actually hit *behind* the ball! In essence you should be producing a slicing action whereby your swingpath goes left of your target, and you hold the club face open (aimed to the right of your swingline) through impact.

You must not ground your club in the sand, so take your grip on the club before entering the bunker by placing your thumbs down a line slightly to the left of the front of the grip. This will give you a club face in an open position, using the same grip as usual.

When taking your stance you are allowed to shuffle your feet into the sand which:
1 Gives you a firm base;
2 Tells you how deep and what texture the sand is.

Position your feet and body on a line 15-20 degrees left of your target with the ball opposite your left heel. This will encourage a steeper swing which travels in a line parallel to your

The set up for bunker shots with the feet shuffled into the sand and a narrow stance.

body's aim – to match your open club face.

You should aim to enter the sand two to three inches before the ball, splash the sand and follow through at at least shoulder height with the weight on your left foot as in other shots.

Below: This picture shows two main faults: the club face is de-lofted and the ball is positioned too far back in the stance.

Left: a greenside bunker shot requires an open club face with the ball positioned forward in the stance.

Hazards

This sequence shows the correct greenside bunker technique. The feet and body should aim left of the target. An early wrist break will allow the club head to travel in an upwards direction on the backswing. Make a long swing, taking sand before the ball and keeping the club face open at the bottom with no hint of stopping at the ball.

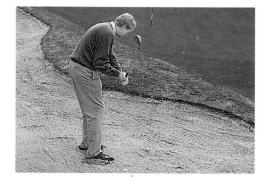

However, unlike other shots you do not want your hands to rotate through impact; your club face must be kept open. Do not allow the toe to pass the heel of the club until after impact, if at all. In playing this shot you should not feel direct contact with the ball. There is a cushion of sand between the club face and the ball which lets you make a long swing but enables the ball to come out slowly.

Practise this shot until you are confident; fear comes only from past failures. You need to be relaxed, and that comes only when you know that you can execute the shot successfully.

Key points

- Open club face – open stance.
- Aim and look at a spot two to three inches behind the ball.
- Take some sand and follow through to shoulder height.

The arms and club should move to the left of the target with the body facing to the left and a long follow through.

Hazards

Playing from a bunker with the ball below the feet as well as a downslope. Adopt a wider stance with more hip bend. The weight should favour the left leg and the club face should be well open. Make an early wrist break to clear the back lip of the bunker, and take 2-3 inches of sand before the ball.

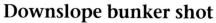

Downslope bunker shot

- Well open club face and stance.
- Aim to hit three to four inches behind the ball.
- Weight more on the left side.
- Club head to follow the contour of the sand with a steeper backswing and lower follow through.

Keep the forward swing low after contact. Your weight must stay on the left leg throughout the swing with no hint of falling back. The trajectory will tend to be low.

- Shorter swing; the ball will come out lower with run.

Upslope bunker shot

- Not so open club face and stance.
- Aim to hit only ½ inch to one inch behind the ball.
- Weight more on the right side.
- Club head to follow the contour of the sand; follow through swings up more quickly.
- Long swing because the ball will pop up higher rather than forwards.

To play an uphill bunker shot, use an open stance with more weight on the right leg. Aim to take less sand before the ball and let the long forward swing follow the contour of the bunker. The ball will come out naturally with a high trajectory.

Hazards

Above: The set up for a long bunker shot. The feet are not shuffled into the sand, and the sole of the club is held level with the ball's equator.

The long bunker shot

To achieve distance from a fairway bunker, firstly you need a flat lie without any ridges of sand just behind the ball. The shot is played in a similar way to a normal fairway shot, but you must ensure that you take the ball first.

● Shorten down on the grip.
● Address the ball halfway up.
● Check that you are selecting a club with sufficient loft to clear the bunker face.

Opposite and left: This shows the correct swing for a long bunker shot. Notice how the arms and club move together to give a wide, sweeping arc.

Inset left: The wrong way to play a long bunker shot. The feet are shuffled into the sand, the ball is too far back, and an early wrist break has been made.

Hazards

Plugged bunker shot
(Top of ball below surface)
● Close club face severely – toed in so that the end of the toe is pointing at the ball.
● Steep takeaway with wrist break.
● Downward jab into the sand and ball, with only one inch of sand before the ball.
● Ball will pop up but will have a lot of topspin; you cannot control this shot.

Note: Always leave the bunker in a well raked condition – the way you would like to find it.

Remember that the ball will fly much lower from this type of lie and contains little or no backspin, so be prepared for it to run much further than normal.

See how the stance for this stroke differs from a normal bunker shot, being much less open with the ball placed back towards the right foot. As you can see from the impact position, there must be no attempt to lean backwards to scoop the ball out of its buried lie. Rather, you must focus on hitting firmly down into the sand trusting the club to explode the ball out.

Hazards

Ball under lip of bunker

Even in a lie such as this one where the ball is close to the overhanging lip of the bunker, the same basic method should be used. What you need here is extra height so place the ball further forward in your stance which effectively increases the loft of your club face. Open your stance a little more than normal and swing in the usual way. The ball will rise very quickly without any need to try to lift it over the lip.

The key thoughts in your set up are: open stance (feet aiming left); club face well open; and position the ball forward in your stance. The club head must be swung up quickly with an early wrist break to a full backswing position. The downswing must be led by the left arm for a sharp downward angle into the sand 2-3 inches behind the ball. The club face must be kept open throughout the forward swing, your hands and the club moving together. There must be no attempt to scoop the ball up. Notice the behind the ball position of the player's head and the continuous line of the left arm and club shaft. Your full follow through will often be restricted by the face of the bunker but by the time you reach this position, the ball has left the bunker and it does not matter if your club hits hard into the bank. Notice how the weight has transferred on to the left leg.

Avoiding water and trees

Many golfers when confronted with a tree-lined course or one with water hazards, tend to panic and see all the trouble and the places they don't want to hit the ball. Always look at the target and visualize the positive shot – where you want to hit the ball and not where you don't want to hit it.

Try to shade out the hazard areas and just visualize the sun shining on the fairway or green, whichever is your target area. Light up your target and see yourself hitting it.

Alas, however positive you are, and the nature of golf being as it is, you will still find positions on the course that are not ideal and which require recovery shots. Don't worry, because once you know how to hit high or low shots bending from right to left or from left to right, it is fun to pull off a recovery.

Only attempt those shots of which you are capable. Don't be unrealistically ambitious. The practice ground is the place to cultivate the more difficult shots in the game.

Right: Positive thoughts are needed when you are playing over water. You should concentrate on making good contact with the ball, and try to blank out any negative thoughts and fears.

Hazards

Moving the ball left to right (fade)

Stand behind the ball and picture your intended ball flight; choose the line on which you want the ball to start. You must build your stance and alignment around this line because the swingpath direction is the most powerful force and dictates where the ball flies initially.

This sequence shows the correct technique for the fade (left-to-right shot). The set-up aim is to the left. Both hands should be adjusted anti-clockwise on the club with the ball just inside the left heel. The top of the backswing position is upright, the arms should swing left with the club face held open on the follow through. The set-up grip change allows the club face to return in an open position, but you should keep the left hand leading. The balls on the ground indicate the flight path of the ball.

In order to impart clockwise spin on the ball to make it bend to the right you will need to select a fairly straight-faced iron – a 4 or 5 is ideal. A lofted club produces backspin which negates the degree of sidespin.

Place both thumbs down on the grip just left of the centre line. When you look down you should see less of the back of your left hand, and more of the back of your right hand than normal. This grip will allow you to feel the club face in a more open position on the backswing and to maintain the open position through impact to create the desired clockwise spin on the ball.

Key points

● Feet and body aim to the left.
● Hands should be positioned further left on the grip.
● Ball should be positioned towards front foot.
● Backswing should be straighter back and up to a more upright position (not so rounded).
● On the follow through, swing your arms across the body to finish left of your left shoulder.
● Don't rush the strike – take a smooth, slow swing.

Hazards

Moving the ball right to left (draw)

Picture the desired ball flight you need to avoid the trees or obstacle while standing behind the ball. Choose the initial line you want, and this becomes your target both for stance and your body alignment.

To produce anti-clockwise spin (right to left) on the ball, you must make contact with a closed club face. Because

The set up for the draw (right-to-left shot). You need a strong grip with both hands adjusted clockwise on the club. The club face should be closed and the ball positioned towards the back of the stance. The feet and body aim to the right. The balls on the ground show the flight path of the ball.

90

closing the club face also reduces the loft, choose a more lofted club than for a fade – a 6 or 7 is ideal.

Your set-up grip should be turned on the club to your right (thumbs right of centre line); as you look down, you will see more of the back of your left hand and less of the back of your right than normal.

Note: The ball will land with overspin causing more run, so allow for this result.

Key points

- Feet and body should aim right.
- Club face should be toed in slightly (closed).
- Hands should be positioned further right on the grip.
- Ball should be positioned towards middle of stance.
- Backswing should be more rounded, on an inside curve.
- Forearms and hands should rotate through impact.
- Follow through towards the initial aim point.
- Don't rush the strike; use a slow, smooth swing.

Hazards

Playing a high shot

Make sure that you select a club that is sufficiently lofted to clear the obstacle. It does not pay to be too greedy and end up in a worse position. Your first priority must always be to 'get the ball back in play'.

Key points

- Ball should be positioned further forwards than normal – more towards your left foot.
- Hands should be level, or just slightly behind the ball.
- Your weight should favour the right leg.
- Make sure that you keep your head still, and behind the ball until after impact.
- Take a divot, and get to the bottom of the ball.

Left: When setting up for a high shot, the ball should be positioned forwards in the stance. The hands should be just behind the ball with the weight favouring the right side.

Playing a low shot

It is possible to use a range of clubs to produce a low ball flight, provided that you reduce the loft by keeping your hands forward of the club head through impact, a 5 or 6 iron is ideal.

Key points

● Ball should be positioned more towards your right foot.

● Hands should be forward of the ball, and level with the middle of your left thigh.

● Club face should be toed in slightly.

● Your weight should favour the left leg.

● Don't hit the shot too hard – it will travel a good distance with little effort. A half to three quarters swing is adequate.

Right : The set up for a low shot. The ball is towards the back of the stance with the hands well forward. Note the shaft angle and the club face with the toe turned in.

Hazards

Uneven stances and lies

To execute a successful shot from a slope, a number of set-up changes need to be made, which are listed here.

Ball above your feet

● Posture should be straighter, with less bend from waist.
● Move hands lower down the club grip.

● Aim a little right of your target.
● Ball should be positioned towards centre of your stance.

To contact a ball that is higher than the level of your feet, you must adopt a flatter more rounded swing on both the backswing and follow through. This swing pattern will tend to produce a right-to-left shot, and hence the aim adjustment to the right at address.

Above: This set up is incorrect. The knees and hips are both too bent and the hands are too low.

The correct set up with the ball above the feet, showing less hip bend and aiming to the right to allow for the likely right to left ball flight. The clubs on the ground show this.

Hazards

Ball above feet

This swing sequence with the ball above the feet shows how your posture should be straighter and the swing plane flatter. The more rounded swing produces a shot that flies from right to left.

Hazards

Ball below your feet

● Posture should be more bent from your **hips**, not knees.
● Aim to the left of your target.
● Use a longer club.
● Ball should be positioned towards your left foot.

Your swing plane will have to be more upright to reach a ball that is below your hips throughout the swing; otherwise you will hit the top of the ball. The ball flight will bend to go from left to right, for which you have allowed already in your set-up aim.

Certain set-up adjustments have to be made when the ball is below the feet. You should bend more from the hips, keeping the back straight. Aim left to allow for left-to-right ball flight as indicated by the balls on the ground opposite.

Above: The incorrect set up with the ball below the feet. There is too much knee bend and insufficient bend from the hips.

Hazards

Ball below feet

This swing sequence shows the ball below the feet. You should bend more from the hips and aim left. Make a more upright backswing and retain the spine angle to stay low through impact. The correct posture will make a balanced follow through possible.

Hazards

Above: An incorrect set up when playing from an upslope. The weight is leaning into the slope and the ball is too far back in the stance.

Right: The correct set up when playing from an uphill lie. Note how the body weight corresponds with the slope; it favours the right leg.

Uphill lie

- Body weight should be parallel with the slope, favouring the right leg.
- Use a less lofted club.
- Aim slightly to the right of your target.
- Position the ball towards your left foot.

Your swing angle into the ball must correspond with the slope, so your follow through must rise more quickly so as not to bury the club into the ground. The slope and your body weight staying back on your right side will cause the ball to fly much higher, and you will tend to pull it to the left – hence your aim adjustment.

Downhill lie

- Body weight should be parallel with the slope, favouring the left leg.
- Right shoulder should feel higher than the left.
- Use a more lofted club.
- Aim to the left of your target.
- Position the ball towards the centre of your stance.

This is a difficult shot to play well; you must not try and lift the ball. Choose a lofted club which becomes less lofted purely by the way in which the slope requires you to stand.

Your club head should start to rise more quickly on the backswing and stay lower after the ball to correspond with the slope. A lower shot will result and there will be a tendency for the ball to fade from left to right.

Do not attempt a straight-faced club off a downslope. A 5 iron is about the longest club you should contemplate using, unless you are very proficient at this shot.

Above: An incorrect set up from a downslope, leaning back into the slope with the ball too far forwards.

Left: The correct set up when playing from a downhill lie. The body weight corresponds with the slope, favouring the left leg.

CHAPTER FIVE

The Short Game
by Craig DeFoy

The average round of golf, whether it is played by a top tournament professional or a high-handicap weekend golfer, is made up from 37 per cent of full shots and 63 per cent of short shots. From these figures it is obvious that a proficient short game brings tremendous rewards. Indeed, it has often been said that a good chipper and putter is a match for anyone.

Whilst the long shots can be dependent to a certain extent on an individual's strength and sense of balance, the short game requires very little of either – rather, the skills needed are touch and feel making it possible for the slightest woman to compete on equal terms with the physically strongest of men.

It is true to say that practising the short game regularly will promote a rapid and noticeable improvement in any golfer's skill level; you have only to note how much time the tournament professionals devote to constantly honing their play on and around the greens.

Confidence is a vital element of successful golf, and a good short game is the cornerstone upon which that confidence is built. If a player is reliable at holing out from a short distance, then there is far less pressure on his putting from a longer distance and therefore he can afford to be more aggressive on the greens. Likewise, good putting eases the pressure on chipping and pitching which, in turn, leads to more relaxed and successful play not only around the greens but also on approach shots. This confidence in our ability to finish a hole strongly encourages us to swing more freely, and therefore effectively, throughout our game and is the basis of good play and consistent scoring.

The short game

Putting

Putting is frequently described as a game within a game, and certainly when you consider that the putter is used on average between 30 and 40 times in every round, then it is obviously the most important part of the game. The difference between winning and losing golf tournaments and competitions can often be traced to the holing or missing of those crucial putts.

Just as there are many ways to swing a golf club successfully, so there are even more methods that golfers employ to putt well. A quick look at the great putters over the years – Bobby

This is the most popular putting grip, certainly amongst professionals and low handicap amateurs. It is known as the reverse overlap and because it allows the hands to work together as one unit, it gives you the ideal combination of feel and control.

Jones, Bobby Locke, Bob Charles, Billy Casper, Arnold Palmer, Gary Player, Jack Nicklaus, Seve Ballesteros and many more – will reveal a myriad of individual styles all of which have proved successful for these superstars of the game. Rather therefore than recommending one style or another, I suggest that you study the different methods and try to find some common features. Incorporating these fundamentals, you can experiment to find the method that suits you best.

All good putters stand comfortably over the ball, and the vast majority hold the putter lightly in order to feel and balance the club better. Most stress the importance of having the eyes directly over the ball at address, and all accelerate the putter head through the ball at impact. Through practice and experi-

ment you will discover your own most effective and comfortable grip, stance and stroke, so let's concentrate on the mystical art of rolling that little white ball into the hole consistently well.

Line and length

There are two elements to every putt – line and length. Both are vital, but the emphasis on short putts is on line, whereas on longer ones it shifts to length. The most common cause of missed putts from a short range is a tendency to try to steer the ball into the

judge, so concentrate your efforts on striking the ball solidly along the correct line. Select a point a few inches in front of the ball on your chosen line and focus on simply rolling the ball over this point. This method will improve your short putting enormously and thereby greatly ease the pressure on your longer putts.

hole, thereby raising the head too early and causing you to quit on the ball and all too often push or pull it wide of the target. From such short distances, the strength of the putt is relatively easy to

Practise putting over a marker placed just in front of the ball like this and your percentage of successful putts from a short range will be high. Note how still the head and body remain in these photographs when the concentration is focused only on starting the ball towards the hole rather than steering the ball into it.

Above: An all too common result; trying to guide the ball into the hole from a short distance will cause too much upper body and head movement and inevitably a missed putt.

The short game

When putting from a long range, don't concern yourself too much with the precise line, but leave this to your instinct; first impressions are generally correct so trust your judgement of line and spend most of your time on trying to gauge the distance. This is by far the more important element of a long putt –

seldom do we misjudge the line by more than a few feet, but rolling a golf ball the correct distance is much more tricky and failure to judge this correctly is the cause of the majority of three-putt greens.

Try walking to a point roughly halfway between the ball and the hole and take a few practice strokes from there. Look to and fro from ball to hole and you'll find your feel for the length of the putt is much improved. Remember, it's only a matter of feel and judgement so don't be over-concerned with technique – trust your eyes and trust your stroke!

Judging the borrow of a putt

Just one more point about putting – how do we learn to estimate the amount of borrow? Since this is largely judgemental, some people will always be more gifted than others, but with a few hints and a little experience, the beginner soon finds that he or she can make rapid improvement.

Obviously, the slower the ball is travelling the more it will be affected by slope and the more borrow it will take. This being the case, you must study the area around the hole carefully since on an approach putt, the ball should be rolling very slowly as it nears the cup and will take any swing that exists. On fast greens it follows that the ball will take more borrow than on slower ones; whereas when greens are wet they are not only slower but also the surface water tends to cause the golf ball to travel straighter than normal.

Sometimes it can seem very difficult to determine the slope on a green, and it can often be helpful to stand back and take note of the lie of the land in the immediate area. Frequently, you will find that the borrow on your putt will be in the same general direction.

Chipping

The straightforward run-up from the fringe of the green is one of the simplest yet most important shots in the game. Too often, people make the stroke over-complicated, but, as in all other golf shots, the simplest way is by far the most effective.

I strongly recommend that the chip shot should be played with either a pitching wedge or a 7 iron. Repeated practice with just these two clubs will quickly enable you to judge accurately the amount of carry and run that you can expect.

The technique employed is identical whichever club is used, except that for the same length of shot the wedge needs to be struck more firmly due to the greater backspin created by the more lofted club.

The set up

When setting up for the chip shot, open your stance as if you are going to bowl the ball underarm towards the hole. This position, as shown in the photograph, is both comfortable and natural and allows the player to judge the line and length much more accurately than from a squarer position. Hold the club towards the bottom of the grip for extra control and stand really close to the ball so that your arms are close to your body. Finally, shift most of your weight on to your left foot and place your hands well in front of the club head.

Right: The set up for a chip shot.

The short game

Playing the shot

You are now in a perfect position to play the chip, and to do so successfully you should think in terms of keeping the club head close to the ground throughout the swing, allowing the wrists to break only slightly in the backswing and making a smooth, unhurried brushing stroke through the ball with the hands leading all the way. As can be seen in the photographs, the shot looks really simple – not unlike a long putt with a more lofted club and allowing the loft on the club face to carry the ball

The shot played in this sequence of photographs is a simple running chip with a 7 iron. Note the comfortable, open stance which makes it easy to judge both distance and direction.

through the air for the short distance necessary.

As long as you can avoid the most common faults of 'scooping' the ball into the air using too much wrist action, or leaning back on the right foot, then a little regular practice will enable you to roll three shots into two around the greens on a regular basis. Keep it simple and your handicap is bound to tumble.

The most important point to observe is the way the hands lead the club face through impact and all the way to the completion of the swing, allowing no flicking of the wrists and simply allowing the loft on the club face to lift the ball slightly.

The short game

Pitching

A great deal of mystique seems to surround the short, fairly high shot that is played around the greens and known to us all as the pitch. Good players make it look so easy, and the tournament professionals appear to put the ball next to the flag almost automatically; yet to the beginner, this stroke is often the cause of much head scratching and bemusement.

These photographs of a pitch shot of about 60 yards illustrate that the swing for a pitch is only a miniature version of the full swing. The same fundamentals apply as for any other golf shot, the only real difficulty being judgement of distance. Note how the hands for this shot reach a position on the backswing equivalent to about 10 o'clock on a clockface, and swing through to about 2 o'clock (as illustrated overleaf on page 114).

Starting out in golf

The confusion seems to arise because although people can understand the technique involved in playing a full shot and are able to cope with the simple chip from just off the edge of the green, the pitch falls not too neatly between these two categories and is often regarded as one of those 'clever half shots' best left to experts. However, the fact is that the pitch from anything between, say, 20 and 100 yards is, after a putt, the most commonly played shot in the game of golf. Therefore a degree of mastery of

The short game

The finish of the pitch shot where the arms have swung through to 2 o'clock.

this shot is absolutely essential if a reduction in handicap is your goal, so let's see if we can unravel some of the mystery surrounding it.

The first thing to understand is that there is no special method to employ when hitting a straightforward pitch. Take as a starting point your swing when playing a full wedge shot; when using the same club to hit the ball lesser distances, what you require is essentially the same swing but less of it! If a full wedge flies 90 yards, for example, then for a pitch of 45 yards you should be aiming to take about half as much swing. The important thing to realise is that the ball must *always* – even for a really short shot – be struck with a smoothly accelerating club head, and that any suggestion of slowing down or 'quitting' on the downswing will result invariably in disaster.

The swing

The easiest way to judge the relationship between length of swing and length of shot is to think in terms of a clockface. If your backswing reaches 10 o'clock then your follow through should finish at 2 o'clock, if the backswing goes to 8 o'clock then the finish ought to occur at 4 o'clock, and so on. With a little practice you will soon be able to judge distances for your own swing using this method and should find it paying dividends on the golf course.

A further point to note from the photographs is that the stance becomes narrower and progressively more open as the length of shot decreases.

Although a very open stance does not work too well on a full swing, it can be beneficial with a shorter one since it will enable you to judge the length of your pitch more accurately.

One question that is always cropping up is: 'How do I achieve more back-spin on these short shots?' The answer is that the ball has to be struck positively and slightly on the downswing which enables the grooves on the club face to do their job and bite into the ball surface thereby creating the necessary spin. Imagine a ball being hit firmly in one direction but being forced to spin at a tremendous rate (up at 10,000 revs per minute for a top pro using a wedge) in the opposite direction, and you can easily see why that ball will stop quickly when it lands on the green. However, generally this amount of spin will be beyond most beginners if only because the pros tend to use the balata covered, wound golf balls, which are not usually used by high handicappers because they cut so easily and therefore prove rather expensive.

Common faults

A word of warning! *Never* lean back on to your right foot when playing a pitch shot in an attempt to scoop the ball high into the air. This is the most common fault and will result only in a fluffed or thinned shot, and the thought of having to play a similar shot all over again is a daunting prospect! Try to trust your swing and allow the loft on your club to create the shot for which it was designed.

The short game

Practise your pitching

Remember the basic rule and whatever else you decide to practise, never neglect your pitching clubs – make them your friends and you will be quickly repaid by better shots and lower scores.

When trying to hit different lengths of bunker shot, resist the temptation to vary the distance you hit behind the ball. Instead, simply adjust the length of your swing, just as you would for a pitch from grass. Even when

A ball in its own pitch-mark

Only when the ball is really deeply embedded in its own pitch-mark in the sand should you alter your method. For this shot the ball is placed opposite the right foot and the backswing is very steep and straight back from the ball in line with the target. Hit firmly down into the sand some 3 or 4 inches behind the ball and make no attempt to follow through. This method will blast the ball

This shot travelled about 35 yards and is another good illustration of our clockface theme. In this instance, the hands have travelled from about 8 o'clock to around 4 o'clock whereas the movements of the legs and upper body are again just a much smaller version of a full golf swing.

the ball has finished close to the lip of the trap and needs to rise steeply, don't attempt to scoop it out. Just stand a little more open with the golf ball even further forward in the stance and trust your swing – have faith because it is possible to make the ball rise almost vertically from this position.

out much lower than normal and with very little backspin, so be prepared for it to run a long way. As you become a little more expert, you will be able to play this shot more effectively but it is always difficult to judge and should be used only in an emergency, especially if you are a beginner.

Remember to keep your swing smooth and unhurried for all pitch shots and allow the loft on your wedge to take care of the flight of the ball.

The short game

The keys to hitting good bunker shots

1 Always use a sand iron – this club is designed specifically to do the job and is an absolute *must* for every golfer.

2 Always play within your limitations – if the shot seems too difficult, take a penalty drop into an easier position within the bunker and don't automatically go for the flag – get out of the

This sequence of photographs shows the method used for the standard bunker shot. This is the swing you should use for all but the most unusual shots from sand. The method has been described fully and can be seen clearly here. The one thing that the photographs cannot show, however, is the smooth and unhurried rhythm used. This smoothness is absolutely vital, so avoid the temptation to force your swing and concentrate on swinging the club head down into the sand and through to the target without rushing at any point in your movement.

bunker and on to the green as easily as possible.

3 Never be tempted to pick the ball cleanly off the surface – it might look easier, but there is almost no margin for error and it is one of the most difficult shots in the game.

4 Finally, when you do go into a bunker, don't panic and don't attempt to lean backwards and lift the ball up and out. Practise the method described and you will overcome your fear and have a very important weapon in your battle against 'Old man Par'.

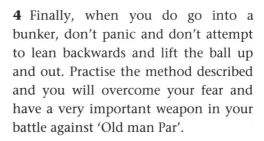

The short game

Pitch shots over greenside bunkers

The pitch shot over a greenside bunker often can strike fear into the average player. This is because we instinctively feel the need to hit the ball with a high, gentle flight in order to stop it quickly.

In fact, most bunkers don't have a high lip and all you need to do is carry the ball past them. Try to ignore the sand and pick out a spot on the green as your landing area. Using the most lofted club in your bag, simply swing at the ball smoothly and strike it crisply forward and down. Keeping the weight more on the left side than usual, as shown in the photographs, will encourage the contact you are seeking.

You are looking for backspin – not height, so trust your swing and the loft

This stroke requires the maximum amount of backswing to give yourself a chance to stop near the pin. Use your sand iron to make use of its great loft and play the shot like any other pitch. Notice how there is no suggestion in these pictures of trying to lift a ball over the bunker, but how the club is swung firmly down and through the ball. Your sand wedge has a loft of between 52 and 60 degrees; more than enough to generate the height and backspin you seek.

on your club to create the shot you are after. Never try to lift the ball into the air – it's a recipe for disaster.

Conclusion

Hopefully, you will have discovered for yourself how important the short game is in golf. It so often makes all the difference between a good and a bad score or winning or losing a match. Although it might be less exciting to practise short shots than long ones, there is no doubt that improvement following practice is much more obvious in your short game. So don't spend all those practice sessions thrashing away with your driver or 5 iron – concentrate instead on your wedge and putter and watch those scores come tumbling down.

CHAPTER SIX

Playing a round

by Craig DeFoy

No sportsman, either amateur or professional, would ever dream of starting a game without first loosening up. Why then should a golfer act differently? Yet consider the typical approach of the average player – a last-minute arrival into the car park with perhaps just enough time for a snatched coffee before rushing on to the first tee ready to give the golf ball a flat-out wallop with the driver. It sounds familiar, but it is hardly designed to be effective in your battle against the course.

The correct way to go about playing a round of golf is to ensure that you are ready both mentally and physically to give of your best. Rather than the hurried dash into the club and on to the course, try to make that extra effort to arrive at the course with a little time to spare. It is so important to be in the right frame of mind to play good golf, so if possible do everything a little more slowly than normal. Drive to the club in a smooth, unhurried fashion and try to arrive 30 to 45 minutes before your allocated tee-off time.

Practice

Use this time to hit a few shots on the practice ground. Take your lead from the experts and warm up gradually, starting with a few wedge shots and gradually working up to hitting some balls with your driving club. Whilst doing this warm-up session, concentrate on swinging smoothly and unhurriedly. Don't worry about power; just try to stay relaxed and settle into a good rhythm.

Make the time now for a few putts on the practice green – and some chip shots, if possible. When putting, resist the temptation of trying to hole out as often as you can – there is time enough for that on the course itself. Instead, try to gauge the speed of the greens by rolling a few putts across the green at no particular target – feel the ball coming off the middle of the putter face and watch the ball roll. This is very important for judging the pace. End the putting practice by holing several putts from a very short distance – don't test yourself. What you are seeking is to build up your feel for the putter and the pace of the greens and also boost your confidence by getting used to the sight and sound of the golf ball dropping into the hole.

You should now be ready in both mind and body to walk slowly to the first tee and test yourself against the golf course. This preparation may not always be possible, but it will prove well worth the effort, so try to be prepared before you play and see the improvement in your ball striking and scoring.

Opposite: Always try to leave time before a game to hit a few practice shots to help you warm up.

Playing a round

Planning is the key

If we were able to stop Nick Faldo, for example, just before he began his backswing on any shot and ask the question "What are you trying to do?", the answer would come in the form of a detailed description of a type and shape of shot, and an exact landing area. In other words, Nick or any other top golfer plans what he intends to do and then forms a very clear mental picture of the ideal shot before even addressing the ball. When standing over the ball, the pros swing almost on automatic pilot, trusting their well-grooved and finely tuned swings to produce the shot they have visualized.

That is all well and good for a top professional you might say, but hardly the way for a beginner to set about hitting good shots. On the contrary, even the beginner should have a clear objective when playing since if your goal is vague, your chances of hitting the ball into the right place must be lower than if you know at least what you are trying to do. Too often we stand over the golf ball and simply hope to make a good swing, assuming that the resultant shot will also be good and end up in the right place. This type of approach is very common but is hardly conducive to good shot making and lower scores.

Course management and strategy

Even the beginner should start to learn golf course management and strategy as soon as he starts to play regularly.

As your skill level improves, so that strategy can be adjusted, but you will soon find that if you plan to play a hole in a certain way, then far more often you will pull off the good shots rather than simply aiming straight and adopting the 'hit and hope' approach. Study the illustrations in this chapter and note how a straightforward attack on a hole is not always the easiest way to reach your goal. Provided that you know roughly how far you are likely to hit the ball with each club and what kind of shot you most often produce, then you can begin to form your own plans for each hole and say goodbye to aimless golf. Vague, hopeful golf just does not work consistently. Use your brains as well as your muscles and see how much better the results are – planning is really the key to rapid improvement in scoring!

Play within your limitations

Probably the biggest mistake regularly made by most golfers – particularly the high handicapper or beginner – is that they attempt to play in a manner that is beyond their capabilities. So often we see a player attempting a brilliant recovery shot only to fail and find himself in even deeper trouble. Far better to realise the limits of his talents and take his medicine; almost invariably the best way to escape from trouble following a poor shot is to take the

Starting out in golf

On this par 3 hole, you should almost always be aiming for the left half of the green which affords a greater margin for error. Only in a desperate situation in matchplay should you consider going directly for the pin.

easiest and quickest route back to the fairway.

Much as this might appear to be thoroughly sensible, it still seems incredibly difficult for most of us to feel able to resist the temptation to try for just that little bit more than we can normally accomplish. Perhaps this is just a normal human reaction, but in the world of golf, it is simply counter-productive to good performance.

Knowing your limitations

This sounds reasonable, but how do we know what our limitations are? First of all, we must know how far we are likely to hit the ball with a given club. To

discover this, take a bag of balls on to the practice ground and hit a number of them with various clubs, pace the distance to your average shot with each one and you have a basis from which to work. Obviously, weather conditions will affect the distance a ball flies, but only experience can teach you to what extent. When you are faced with a shot over a hazard, you then have some concrete information to work with and not just guesswork.

Next, consider a situation where you are faced with a shot from a tight lie over a greenside bunker with very little green with which to work. Common sense suggests that the novice player is hardly likely to play the shot of a life-

Playing a round

Safety first on par 3's

A beginner is unlikely to score many threes during his round and obviously the par 3's offer the best opportunity. However, frequently these holes can prove a minefield for the unsuspecting golfer. If the hole is not too long, we can often be tempted to go recklessly for the flag which seldom pays off.

On this hole, you should almost always be aiming for the left half of the green where even a poor shot leaves a chance of a three. Only in a desperate situation in matchplay should you consider going directly for the pin since there is almost no margin for error.

time, so why try? Many beginners seem to have a blinkered approach to this game – only the flag seems to exist and the most direct route to it! Instead of a forlorn attempt at a career shot, why not play a simpler shot to a position on the green from where you can get down in two putts. Heroics should be attempted

only in a desperate matchplay situation and not as a matter of course.

If you often find yourself surrounded by trees following yet another errant tee-shot, surely a 'do or die' attempt to thread the ball through a distant and narrow gap from a less than perfect lie is madness? If not,

Weigh up the odds

There are two obvious ways to play the hole illustrated here; the black route is the attacking one which would no doubt be used by a professional or low-handicap player. Even a less experienced player could tackle the hole in this way but only if he is certain of his ability to clear the ditch with his tee-shot.

If this were an early hole in the round when perhaps you are not fully loosened up, or later if your swing is not performing as well as it should, then the second route could be the one to take.

Playing up short of both the ditch and green would then leave an easy pitch to the flag giving you a good chance of a four, but if not an almost certain five.

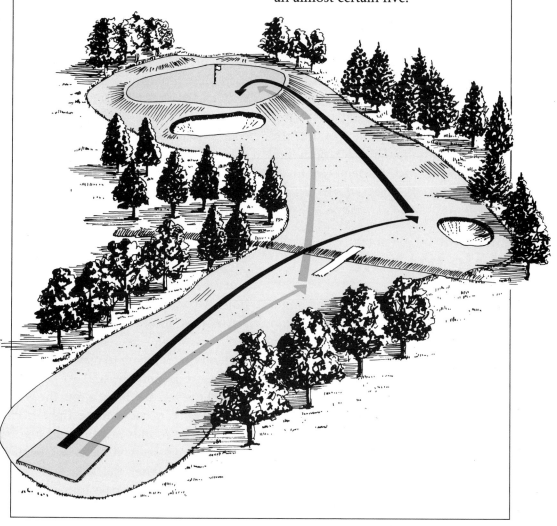

Playing a round

then why are you so often in this predicament having missed the fairway when the ball was sitting on a peg on a perfectly prepared tee ground? It is hardly sensible, but human instinct seems to lead us to this course of action. Although these observations may seem to suggest that a defensive policy is best, this is not always true. If you have a good chance of success, by all means go for the shot, but if the odds are stacked against you – be sensible. Only attempt to do what you can reasonably expect to accomplish – this is realistic and positive thinking and can only help in your efforts to improve your scoring.

A beginner is unlikely to score many threes during his round and obviously the par 3's offer the best opportunity. However, frequently these holes can prove a minefield for the unsuspecting golfer. If the hole is not too long, you may be tempted to go recklessly for the flag which seldom pays off.

Hole by hole

Whilst for the most of us the main reason for playing golf is to have fun and enjoy the challenge of pitting ourselves against the course, we are still not satisfied with hitting the ball well if it means that our good shots are not reflected in the overall score. This pressure, often just self-inflicted, to produce a satisfactory end result can frequently have an adverse effect on our efforts to play well during our round. If we are constantly aware of the state of our score compared with our handicap or par, then we are not really in a position to concentrate fully on the shot in hand.

This ability to play just one shot at a time need not belong only to the champions of the game, and yet so often it can mean the difference between good and bad play. Even for a beginner at the game, it quickly becomes obvious that our failure to forget that earlier missed putt or bad bounce into trouble can seriously affect our concentration on the strike in hand. Likewise, it is so difficult to ignore the thought of that relatively easy par 5 to come with its possibility of a par or even a birdie, or that long, tough par 3 or 4 with its suggestion of even more problems.

The tendency to think in terms of your overall progress in scoring is totally counter-productive so you must learn to play each shot or certainly each hole separately. The time to consider your score for the round is at the *end* of that round, so why waste your energy on worrying or comparing your efforts with previous games?

A round of golf comprises 18 holes, and the better you are able to keep those holes separate, the more fruitful your attempts at good scoring and handicap reduction will be. Nobody would pretend that it is easy to play in this way because it is only natural to want to know how you are doing along the way, but if you can concentrate right from your earliest rounds of golf on trying to see each and every hole as a separate entity, then the quicker you will progress in your struggle to master the game.

Most of the time spent playing a round of golf is taken up not by hitting the ball but by walking after it or searching for it! This time between shots is in many ways the most crucial part of the game. If you become too obsessive with your scoring, then the strain just becomes too much and your game is likely to collapse. Try therefore to empty your mind after each shot, take the opportunity to enjoy the surroundings – listen to the birds, look at the trees – and remember, you could be working!

Above all else, golf is a social game allowing all kinds of people from different backgrounds and with different levels of ability to play together. Don't lose sight of this fact. By all means concentrate on your shots, but between times, relax and soak up the atmosphere, enjoy the company of your fellow golfers and remember – a golf score is made up from a number of strokes all of an identical value; rather like building a wall, the end product is only as good as the placing of each individual brick.

Right from the start of your golfing career: stroke by stroke and hole by hole – that's the way to build your score!

Par is negotiable

All golf holes have a nominated value of 3, 4 and 5 which is known as par. Par is decided basically by the length of a hole as follows:

Par 3 - holes of 250 yards and under.
Par 4 - holes from 251 to 475 yards inclusive.
Par 5 - holes of 476 yards and over.

Quite recently, however, the degree of difficulty has come to be used as a further criterion. For instance, a long par 4 could be just below the required distance but if it played steeply uphill then the hole could be termed a par 5. Similarly, if a hole had a feature such as a stream or lake in front of the green which made it unlikely that the majority of players could reach the green with their second shots, then that hole could be allocated a par of 5.

Two world-famous examples can be found in the Augusta National Course in Georgia made so familiar to all golfers by the US Masters Tournament played each April and beamed to a worldwide television audience. The beautiful 13th at Augusta is only a par 4 according to its length but due to its difficulty has always been a par 5, whereas the 10th is more than long enough to be considered a 5 but as it is played steeply downhill all the way from tee to green, it has always been played as a par 4.

The whole handicapping system of golf is based on a player's score in relation to the par of the course, so this is the common method whereby we can measure our ability. Furthermore, much of the terminology of the game such as birdie, eagle, bogey etc. is related to the par figure of the hole in question. The beauty of the system is that unlike other sports, players of widely differing abilities are able to compete with each other on equal terms. There can, however, be a drawback to each hole having a predetermined value in that we all feel under pressure to play that hole to a standard

Playing a round

Don't play in blinkers

This long par 5 shows two distinct routes to the hole. On the one hand, you can see the typically blinkered approach taken by even some very good golfers. Alternatively, the less direct approach is far more sensible and is a good example of a thinking man's strategy.

By taking the direct route you risk going into the fairway bunker and leave yourself with a testing third shot to the flag. Playing into the wide areas of the fairway, however, would not only be safer but would offer a much easier pitch and would certainly be more likely to earn the par you seek.

Think before you hit

Here we have a typical par 4 where an opportunity is presented for a really spectacular drive across the corner of the dog leg which would leave a much shorter second shot to the green.

The odds on pulling off such a shot, however, are too long to make it worthwhile. The common sense strategy here is to take a shorter club from the tee towards the fairway bunker and well away from the trees. The green is now opened up for your second shot which should be aimed into the relatively wide central area, thereby not having to play over the greenside trap.

preset for us. Because the par is defined mainly by distance and we don't all hit the ball the same way, the shorter hitters always seem to be labouring at a disadvantage and they can often be tempted to swing harder than they should just to play the hole as it is set out officially.

This pressure can be eased by each player working out the par on every hole on his or her course based on personal ability in terms of their own achievable distance. The par of a hole of 470 yards may be 4 but most high handicappers would struggle to reach the green in two

Playing a round

shots. However, if we see the hole as a par 5, then we can approach it in a more relaxed fashion since we are now allowed three shots to reach the green. Working out the course hole by hole in this way based on an individual's best likely performance will give us a much higher total par figure but is a much more realistic standard by which a high handicapper or beginner can judge his performance.

As the golfer's experience increases and his skill level improves, so he can lower his personal par for the course. In this way we can measure our improvement and at the same time avoid the danger of trying too hard and too soon to achieve an unrealistic target.

This outlook on scoring has proved highly successful for golfers of all categories, so why not give it a try and see whether it could work for you too!

Take your medicine

Despite the very best of preparation, planning and even the best of swings, golf balls will always find a way to miss the fairways or greens and plummet into the rough, trees or hazards. Although you sometimes get lucky breaks in terms of good lie and a clear view to the fairway or green, most often you are faced with a recovery shot back on to the prepared surface of the course. In this situation there is a golden rule: *take your medicine*. In other words, accept the fact that you have dropped a stroke and take the shortest, safest route possible back to the short grass.

It is often hard to accept this approach because your first instinct is to retaliate against your ill fortune and try to make up for it by playing a dare-devil, make or break stroke to the accompaniment of cries of disbelief from your playing partners – what a massive boost to the ego and all so tempting. Consider, however, how you came to be in this situation in the first place – your failure to hit a successful shot from a good lie on the fairway or a perfect one from the tee. How then can you expect to thread a ball through a narrow gap in the branches from a less than perfect lie in the rough? Unrealistic maybe, but it is still an ever present temptation, certainly for the majority of golfers. After all, it is frequently the one exciting shot of the day that we remember best and the one that brings us back for more the following week regardless of our overall play and score.

However, for every time such a stroke succeeds, on far more occasions it is doomed to failure. This being the case, try to be objective when you find yourself in trouble and weigh up the odds on success or failure, and only when these odds are well and truly in your favour should you play the risky shot. If you decide to go for it, do so in a whole-hearted and confident manner. If you have considered the options, you are hardly being rash or foolhardy.

Generally speaking, however, damage limitation is the name of the game so try to remember the golden rule – *take your medicine* and get back onto the short grass! It will pay dividends in the long term by helping to get rid of those disastrous holes and bringing a measure of consistency to your scoring.

Analyse for improvement

Your round is over and what have you learned? First of all, golf is difficult – surely the most difficult of all sports! Secondly, the surroundings in which you play the game are probably the most relaxing and interesting sporting grounds that exist. Mostly, however, you have experienced the challenge to your physical and mental abilities that golf demands above all other games. The frustration created by your bad shots and the pure exhilaration you enjoy when your labours are rewarded by a good one are what golf is all about.

What then can you do to improve and how can you learn from your experience? Obviously, practising the golf swing and improving your technique is part of the answer, but if you are not careful, it is all too easy for you to practise in a haphazard fashion, in which case your improvement will be slow.

Deciding what area of your game needs most work is really very logical – which clubs do you know you will use most frequently during a round – certainly the putter, but also the wedge and driving club, so obviously you must practise with these constantly to develop familiarity and confidence.

We are all different, however, so try to acquire the habit of analysing your rounds of golf as soon as possible after their completion. Perhaps as you are driving home from the course, a little quiet reflection on how your game went would do some good.

Better still, why not produce a chart? Mark yourself honestly out of ten for each department of the game. This will identify immediately your current strengths and weaknesses, making it obvious which clubs you should concentrate your efforts on for the next short while. Keep your chart pinned on the inside of your locker or perhaps the back of a door at home and update it on a regular basis – perhaps every three to four weeks. Your objective should be to raise the marks for each department to a consistently high level by which time you should have noticed quite an improvement in your scoring as well as your ball striking. One word of warning! When first making your chart, don't dwell too much on the low marks – try congratulating yourself on those parts of the game in which you score highly. Self-esteem breeds confidence.

Concentrating your energy where it is needed most can only help to speed your progress towards lower scores, but don't allow yourself to become too engrossed in the result; golf is after all only a game and if we cease to enjoy playing the game for its own sake then we lose the point of playing at all!

CHAPTER SEVEN

The Mental Game

by Craig DeFoy

It is often said that golf is a game of inches – quite true when we consider that a one inch putt has the same value as a 300 yard drive. The most important inches, however, are the few between the ears! Golf differs from most ball games in that it is played with a stationary ball. Although, at first, this makes the game sound easier, we are all aware that just the opposite is true.

When we play a moving ball game, a great deal of reaction is involved with little time for thought or planning. Golf, on the other hand is played at the pace of the individual player – the stationary ball waiting to be struck only when the golfer is ready. Jack Nicklaus has often stated that he never hits a shot until he is absolutely ready, but how many average golfers can say the same? Nicklaus is aware that if his mental state is not perfect he cannot expect his body to create a successful shot.

You may well argue that what is vital for the best players may not really be relevant for the beginner. However, if the most talented players with the best mechanics consider the condition of their minds to be crucial, then surely those of us who are less talented physically cannot afford to ignore it.

What kind of mental state should you be seeking for golf? The answer is one of calm and awareness in which you are able to focus your attention on the task in hand without getting over-excited or 'pumped up'. Equally, you want to be able to ignore distractions such as over-talkative playing partners or other outside disturbances. Many years ago, a famous lady player was preparing to putt during an important event when a train passed by on a nearby railway track. Without seeming to notice, she holed her putt, and later when asked how she retained her concentration, she replied, "What train?" This may be an extreme example but how much easier golf would be if you could shut yourself off from all such distractions and simply get on with your own game.

Most players have experienced a state in which they were able to concentrate easily, where they were aware of outside agencies but not put off by them, and where they seemed to be able to swing slowly and easily, pulling off shots without their normal amount of effort. They talk of their ability to 'picture' a shot before playing it and of how much simpler the game appears to be when they are in this mood.

This condition of the mind and body has been called many things by many golfers, but perhaps Timothy Gallway in his book *The Inner Game of Golf* described it best, calling it 'the awareness mode'.

To be able to slip into such a condition at will is the dream of all top golfers and other athletes and takes a great deal of understanding, time and practice.

Two heads or one? Two heads are nearly always better than one. Nick Faldo and Ian Woosnam seemed completely in tune with each other and formed an unbeatable team at the 1989 Ryder Cup.

The mental game

Knowing that this calm, controlled state is what we are seeking, however, allows us to recognise that an excited or 'pumped up' approach caused by anticipation of a good round is unlikely to bring the right results. Likewise, being too hard on ourselves when things go wrong, as inevitably they must, causes us to let the mind wander into self pity, a distraction we can do without.

Forget the passion and determination that go into other sports, and try to approach every game of golf in a mood of quiet calm ready to accept whatever comes and determined to think about only one shot at a time.

Concentration

Having identified the state of mind best suited to golf, there is a very important word to consider: concentration. What is concentration? How do we define it? Mental calmness is all very well but you still need to focus on each shot as it comes along and to do this successfully each shot has to be interesting. If an object or event is of interest, then you can become absorbed easily and focus your attention on it naturally. This seems to be a reasonable definition of concentration: a state during which your attention is focused upon one thing to the exclusion of all else.

The culture in which we live tends to equate concentration with a furrowed brow and intensive stare, and yet if we hark back to our school days, the lessons we remembered were generally those we enjoyed, when we did not need to be told to *try* to concentrate. If we have to try to concentrate, we are not going to

succeed because we have insufficient interest in that subject at that particular moment.

This introduces another important point – for how long can we stay sufficiently interested during a round of golf? If the average round takes between three and four and a half hours, then it is patently unreasonable to maintain a high level of concentration for that length of time. Very little of the total time on the course is actually spent hitting the ball – only three to four minutes in fact. So to concentrate only for that short period does not sound too demanding.

Use the time spent walking between shots to relax and enjoy the social elements of golf – your playing partners and the surroundings, for instance – and only start to think about your next shot as you approach the ball. The hardest thing in the game is to keep your mind on what is happening right now; not what caused that last bad hole or worrying about some previous experience with this particular club or this particular hole perhaps. Equally, you must not race ahead to what may or may not happen in the future. As you approach the golf ball, begin to take note of the various stimuli that affect the upcoming stroke: check the lie and the target area, and calculate how the prevailing weather conditions will affect the flight of the ball? Allow your interest in these stimuli to develop so that by the time you are ready to swing, your attention is focused on now and only now!

Once the ball is on its way, there is nothing you can do to alter its path, so

Crowds? What crowds? This is a scenario to strike terror into a club golfer but for Wayne Grady putting at Troon in the 1989 British Open, the vast crowd hardly exist.

don't waste mental energy on it. Relax, switch your mind on to other things and give your brain a little respite – you will be needing it again soon enough! Learning to switch on and off in this way ensures that your system does not become overloaded and your interest in each shot is maintained more easily. This is much less stressful than 'trying to concentrate' for several hours at a stretch. Remember that golf is a game to be enjoyed – stay interested and concentration will come naturally. So will better golf!

The learning process

There are several ways of learning any process but, over the years, the golf swing has been studied and written about in such detail that it can now seem so complicated as to be impossible to learn. It is doubtful if the original champions of the game really studied their movements to any great extent – somehow the thought of Old Tom

The mental game

Morris describing his golf swing in graphic detail does not ring true. Yet, despite the ancient equipment these players used, they were nevertheless highly competent. Who knows how they would have really compared with today's stars, complete with graphite shafts and all the other high technology now available?

The basic golf swing has changed little from those early days and the basic fundamentals still hold true. The overall shape of the swing remains similar, and the whole movement is basically still about rhythm and hand and eye coordination. Most early instruction was pretty straightforward and, in the absence of high speed photography which enables us to freeze the golf swing in various stages, learning was based principally on observation and imitation. This meant that the swing was seen and learnt as a complete movement rather than as a series of positions, and even now, this can often be the best way to learn to play.

We are far more responsive to a single mental image than a long list of highly technical instructions. The fact that the average golf swing takes only about two seconds to perform makes this point even more graphically! When learning therefore, once we have mastered the basic positions of address, top of backswing, impact and finish, it is far more beneficial for us to visualize the swing as a whole rather than to concentrate on the rhythm that is natural to each individual.

Children are natural mimics and this enables them to learn both quickly and well. Adults create too many barriers when under instruction – they are often frightened of failing or looking inadequate. Children have fewer preconceptions and hang-ups and are able to let go mentally and allow themselves to learn by copying and trial and error. Their minds are like blank sheets of paper and seek only answers, not pitfalls.

The more you allow yourself to observe good golfers and to absorb the image of good swings, the quicker you are going to learn. It is a fact that recalling the image of an expert at bunker play, for example, and then simply playing your own shot without questioning how, will often result in a far better than usual escape from the sand.

Use this imagery rather than trying to follow detailed technical instruction and you will almost certainly discover that golf is a much easier game and a lot more fun too!

Keep it positive

Most people are optimistic by nature. Certainly most golfers are eternal optimists – we have to be! Negative instruction therefore is not the best way forward for most of us. We have seen how concentration is based upon interest in a subject, and the best way to learn a new technique or how to correct an old one is to make it interesting.

Looked at in the context of golfing instruction, it follows then that a single positive idea is far more beneficial than a series of negative commands issued from your brain to your body.

'Don't move your head', for